W0082481

Hallelujahs & HICCUPS

100 Days Devotional Journal

KARA BARKER

Hallelujahs & Hiccups: 100 Days Devotional and Prayer Journal

©2020 by Kara Barker

All rights reserved. No portion of this book may be reproduced, stored in a retrieval system, or transmitted in any form or by any means electronically, mechanically, photocopy, recording, scanning, or other except for brief quotations in critical reviews or articles, without written permission of the publisher.

Published in McKinney, Texas, by Takman Publishing, Inc.

Scripture quotations are taken from the Holy Bible, New International Version®, NIVâ, New King James Version®, NKJV® New American Standard Bible®, NASB®, Copyright® 1973, 1978, 1984 by Biblica, Inc.® Used by permission of Zondervan. All rights reserved worldwide. www.zondervan.com The "NIV" and New International Version" are trademarks registered in the United States Patent and Trademark Office by Biblica, Inc.®

Print ISBN: 978-1-09832-479-7

Introduction

When life becomes overwhelming, we tend to forget the hallelujah moments. Hallelujah moments are those moments that you know without a shadow of doubt that it was God that intervened on your behalf, changed the direction, changed a heart, changed a decision or in some cases busted open multiple doors in the hallway for you to choose like a buffet. The smallest things in our life are usually the most important and the things we feel that were epic hiccups usually are things we can recover from. If you are still breathing, I'm sure you probably have experienced your share of hallelujahs and hiccups. Hiccups will come and go and bring a ray of emotional stresses with them like fear, disappointment, uncertainty, anxiety, depression, rage and mistrust. It's all part of your journey towards spiritual growth. I've had a lot of moments where all I could say is "Thank you Jesus and Hallelujah" for bringing me through and keeping me. Life is not a sprint; it is a marathon and during this run you will have to go through a lot of different things but take comfort in knowing you don't have to do it alone. We were made for community. We're all created for a specific reason and it's up to us to figure out how we maximize our moments to fulfill our God-given potential. We all will have hallelujah and hiccup moments in our life but it all depends on how you frame it and grow through it.

DAY 1
Start Something New

The way you get over the failures from your past is by creating an amazing present. It's time to be brave enough to start something new. What's the worst thing that could happen? I'm not suggesting that you make irrational or unwise decisions, just start by putting yourself out there to see what you can really do. It's easy to stay in a rut and continue your same old mundane routine. Consider a change of pace. It can be as simple as taking a new route to work one day, using the stairs instead of the elevator, going to a different grocery store or even trying seafood. Ok, that's a stretch. Maybe not seafood, yuck! I'm not a fan at all. I guess it's a smell and texture thing. Back to focus. Trying something new opens up the possibility for you to enjoy new things and gain a new perspective on life. Entire careers and life paths are carved out by people dipping their toes into the deep end of the pool and suddenly discovering a love for something they had no idea about. My husband tells me all the time, "The biggest room in the world is room for improvement." Trying new things really can be a small step toward a self-improvement renovation project. And who doesn't need a little self-improvement in their life?

Isaiah 43:19 For I am about to do something new. See, I have already begun! Do you not see it? I will make a pathway through the wilderness. I will create rivers in the dry wasteland.

. . . .

. . . .

. . . .

. . . .

. . . .

. . . .

Prayer:

Lord, give me the courage to step outside of what is safe and comfortable as I trust You to cover me with your all-sufficient grace. Holy Spirit, teach me how to grow my capacity to handle life's challenges from a posture of trust and expectation of good. Thank You for Your faithfulness to me, even when I don't see it. You are my refuge and my strength and with You, all things are possible!

DAY 2
Be Lit

Having the right attitude is a game-changer. It's a temperature gauge. It's the beam of light in a dark moment. Every day is an opportunity to set the tone for people around you in how you interact and engage with others. It's easy to get caught up in your feelings and allow others to hijack you but you are called to be salt of the earth and the light of the world. Jesus said, "Let your light shine before others" (Matthew 5:16a). He explained that no one lights a lamp just to hide it under a basket. A lamp is meant to be placed on a stand to give light to everything around it. Whether you're timid or outgoing, you're called to be a light to the people around you. No one has the power to dim your light or steal your joy. Stop giving people and other things dominion over you. You have greatness within you. You are royalty. Let your light shine and expose the darkness around you. You can't have light and dark at the same time. Be the sun on a rainy day, so a rainbow can appear.

Day

2

· ·

· ·

· ·

· ·

· ·

· ·

· ·

Prayer:

Lord, help me to be a light so others who are lost will be drawn towards You. Help me show mercy and grace through my attitude and help be a reflection of Your unconditional love. In Jesus' Name, Amen.

Transformation

Many people want to change parts of their lives that brought about pain or disappointment. Others prefer to transform their lives by making significant, lasting changes. Transformation happens when your desire to live your new life replaces your desire to live your old life. Transformation acknowledges that you are a pile of fragmented pieces but over time with commitment you can become an amazing masterpiece. Be committed enough to make the necessary time for wholeness. The word of God is transforming. Our thoughts are powerful, and the truth is, you can't have a positive life with a negative mindset. Learning to have the mind of Christ and leaning on His word is essential to being transformed into the person you were originally created to be. Transformation is a constant renewing process that regenerates is self when you fully commit to change. It is not easy and sometimes it is downright painful, but sometimes that is the price of becoming the authentic you. Your mind is a battlefield, but you have access to the Holy Spirit, and He can help you transform from an unknown and uncanny caterpillar into an amazing butterfly.

Proverbs 23:7 For as a man thinks within himself, so he is. He says to you, "Eat and drink!"
But his heart is not with you.

· ·

· ·

· ·

· ·

· ·

· ·

· ·

Prayer:

Lord, awaken my spirit and allow me to be open to change and transformation. Allow my mindset to shift and refocus on what is good, lovely, pure and noble. I'm a willing vessel Lord. Use me in a mighty way. In Jesus' name. Amen.

DAY 4
Courage Over Comfort

Regardless of our hesitation or fear, humans need change to be happy. Try to do something you've never done every single day. Don't be afraid to try new things, color outside the lines and get in the discomfort zone. If you want something you've never had, you have to do something you've never done. It might not always seem like it but the decisions we make every day can influence whether or not we face anxiety, disappointments and stress or peace, happiness and success. Courage is the willingness to make those decisions every day and live face to face with their outcomes. Everyone experiences fear, doubt, depression, and anxiety. But not everyone has the courage to move beyond life's setbacks. Nelson Mandela once said," I learned that courage was not the absence of fear, but the triumph over it. The brave man is not he who does not feel afraid, but he who conquers that fear."

Joshua 1:19 Have I not commanded you? Be strong and courageous. Do not be afraid; do not be discouraged, for the LORD your God will be with you wherever you go.

. . . .

. . . .

. . . .

. . . .

. . . .

. . . .

. . . .

Prayer:

Lord, help me to be bold and courageous and not settle for mediocrity because of fear. Help me conquer every setback, hiccup or life's challenges in Jesus' name, Amen.

The Pivot

If not now, when? You were called to be a game-changer in the kingdom of God. You are called to be a difference-maker in someone's life. If it's not pushing you towards your purpose then it's an assigned detour. The pivot is more of a state-of-mind to ask yourself, "What's working? What do I want to do next?" For many years I have been conditioned to believe that there is a certain order to success in climbing the corporate ladder. I have to say there have been many opportunities that I dodged but also some opportunities that were game changers. I remember about 12 years ago, there was a person in leadership that told me that your career climb is not always going to be a direct path but there may be opportunities where you need to move laterally, backwards or forwards. It's simple, a pivot is doubling down on what is working to make a purposeful shift in a new, related direction. I encourage you to get into a rhythm of evaluating and self-reflecting on what's working best, what you want to do next, what skills you need to develop, what connection is required, and what would be a small win for you. There is power in making purposeful pivots!

Deuteronomy 31:6 Be strong and of good courage, do not fear nor be afraid of them; for the LORD your God, He is the One who goes with you. He will not leave you nor forsake you.

Psalm 27:1 The LORD is my light and my salvation; Whom shall I fear?

. . . .

. . . .

. . . .

. . . .

. . . .

. . . .

. . . .

Prayer:

Lord help me be bold and courageous. Let me be open to new challenges that are outside of my comfort zone. Open new doors and grant me the wisdom to know it's Your will and not my own. In Jesus' name. Amen.

You Are Enough

You are enough. Let me repeat myself again, You are enough. You are capable, you are smart, you are valuable, you are unique, you were fearfully and wonderfully made by the Most High! So what, you didn't get selected, you didn't get the promotion, you didn't get approved, you didn't get elevated, you didn't make the team, you didn't get a call, you didn't make the shot, you didn't get recruited, you didn't get the opportunity. You know why? Because it wasn't your time. But you're still enough. God's power is most effective when all we can do doesn't cut it. He proves Himself more than enough in our weakest moments, directing our steps and carrying our heaviest challenges through to completion. Girlfriend, embrace your true identity and rest from striving to do the impossible and allow God to win the battle for you. You will never be enough to fight some of the treacherous battles you face. You were not equipped to do so anyway. But here is the good news, you have an army of angels backing you up and they don't know how to lose. All you need is all you have. Be still and allow God to fight for you.

Isaiah 58:11 And the LORD will guide you continually and satisfy your desire in scorched places and make your bones strong; and you shall be like a watered garden, like a spring of water, whose waters do not fail.

Philippians 3:7 But whatever was gain to me I count as loss for the sake of Christ.

· ·

· ·

· ·

· ·

· ·

· ·

· ·

Prayer:

Lord help me to see that I am enough because my value and my identity is found in You. Who I am is not what friends, family members, co-workers, supervisors, teachers say I am. What matters is who You say I am. My joy is found in You. Amen.

Count to 10

Life is a journey. So instead of rushing through it, take time to cherish the moments you are given. There are times in which we are like pole vaulters jumping from one mountain to another, without securing a good plant in the ground before taking lift off. The higher the altitude, tenser pressure you will feel on your ability to breathe. I remember when I was working in Human Resources. I was assigned to write a large strategic transition plan and my supervisor took complete credit for all of my work and even removed my name from the documents. She was recognized because of my hard work, and I just remained silent while burning with anger and resentment. After hearing the news about her promotion, on my commute home, I began to reflect and ask myself a few questions. Did her promotion disqualify me from a future promotion? Does she have that much power to hijack my feelings? Was this a battle for me to fight or a leadership lesson on what not to do? When I think about it, the situation stings every once in a while. At the time I was on a 10+ emotionally but at that moment I couldn't do anything but just seek God for clarity and understanding. God sent some valuable allies my way that helped me process the situation while preparing to avoid another situation. One of the quick things I incorporated was mindful pauses and slowly counting to 10 before responding. I wanted to go off, but I had to pause and think a little more strategically. At that moment I had to literally slow down to breathe and enjoy the blessings that were still around me. I began to breathe in good thoughts and release the bad ones. It wasn't easy but if I hadn't encountered that experience, I would have thought it was an acceptable business practice. The funny thing about that situation was some of those allies were in a meeting with that supervisor while she was presenting my work, and it was obvious that she didn't know anything about the ins and outs, so they requested for me to come into the meeting to explain the details. As a continuous learner, I have realized that sometimes counting to ten is a distraction that God gives you to get you out of the way while He works out the equation and solves the problem.

Psalms 118:24 This is the day that the Lord has made; let us rejoice and be glad in it.

. . . .

. . . .

. . . .

. . . .

. . . .

. . . .

. . . .

Prayer:

Lord, help me enjoy each and every moment you give me because my days are not promised. Allow me to rejoice in every season regardless of the circumstances. In Jesus' Name, Amen.

Life's Sour Moments

I have experienced some really sour moments in the past. Things didn't work out as planned and they really left a sour taste in my mouth. However, it is easy to settle and accept the cards that you're dealt and agree with life's sour moments. Or you can add water along with a little sugar to those experiences and make lemonade. Every day has the potential of being new and sweet if you decide to shift your perspective and take those sour thoughts captive. I'm not saying everything is going to be freshly squeezed lemonade but learning how to accept God's delays as not His denial. There is purpose behind every open and closed door. It may be closed because it's not your time nor was it your door, or it was open because there is a mission waiting for you on the other side. How we respond to these moments whether sweet or sour will indicate our ability to take on more responsibilities. Nothing just happens. Until you really understand that, you will try to force open every door and window that should be closed. If you're a believer, you know that God loves you and He knows what is good for you.

Life's sour moments are designed to help you build your faith and perseverance. Now don't get me wrong, the sour moments are not always enjoyable but like chewing on a Sour Patch Kids candy, the initial taste is sour but if you chew it for a while it will turn sweet. There are sweet lessons behind every sour one, just wait and see.

2 Corinthians 10:5 We demolish arguments and every pretension that sets itself up against the knowledge of God, and we take captive every thought to make it obedient to Christ.

Colossians 3:2 Set your minds on things above, not on earthly things.

Day

. . . .

. . . .

. . . .

. . . .

. . . .

. . . .

. . . .

Prayer:

Lord, help me take every thought captive. Help me focus on You alone. Fill my mind with Your truth. In Jesus' Name. Amen.

Prison Break

It is time to break out of the prison in your mindset. A closed mind will never walk through open doors. We must fix our mindset. You will never grow if you stay in your box and color within the lines. Growth requires taking action first. Whether that's adopting a new attitude or a new way of thinking, or literally taking a new direction. There's an old saying that says, "it's not how good you are but how good you want to be." It's time to truly embrace the idea that if you want to break old habits, you must remain fully committed to the process. Whether it's building a new skill, learning a new language, or creating a new path, having the growth mindset will be your winning recipe for change. Sometimes you just need to believe in yourself again and break out of the comfort zone and draw outside of the lines. Use the color purple instead of black. Where the greatest opposition is lies the greatest growth. If you are a worrier by nature, I have good news for you. You have tremendous prayer potential. It's time to break out of your shell and Be GREAT!

Philippians 4:8 Finally, brothers, whatever is true, whatever is honorable, whatever is just, whatever is pure, whatever is lovely, whatever is commendable, if there is any excellence, if there is anything worthy of praise, think about these things

· ·

· ·

· ·

· ·

· ·

· ·

· ·

Prayer:

Lord, all I want is You. Let the truth of Your word consume my thought life! Amen.

Marathon or Sprint... You Choose

I'm not a runner, but I want to be. I'm more like an average mall walker on a good day.

We were all created to run our race and finish our course. In order to do so we need to have a clear vision for every area of our lives. I admit, there are days when the marathon of life is too much to handle. We can easily take on the sprinter's mindset speeding through life and hoping the challenging situations we face will be merely a blur. But life has a way of slowing you down, because you were not created to run all by yourself, there are other people in your life's relay race that depend on you. As you grow as a believer, you will be given different batons to carry. Like the baton of your child telling you they're dropping out of college or the baton of getting laid off from your job or the baton when your spouse tells you they don't love you anymore. Then there's the baton of depression, worry, doubt and low self-esteem. If you're feeling weary and don't feel like running anymore, let me remind you that greater is He that is in you than he that is in the world. You are not alone, and you will win if you keep putting one foot in front of the other. It's your race so pace yourself, take the time, celebrate the small victories, stay the course, get off the course, get back on but keep your eyes focused on the prize. You got this!

2 Timothy 4:7 I have fought the good fight, I have finished the race, I have kept the faith.

Isaiah 4:30 but those who hope in the LORD will renew their strength. They will soar on wings like eagles; they will run and not grow weary; they will walk and not be faint.

. . . .

. . . .

. . . .

. . . .

. . . .

. . . .

. . . .

Prayer:

Lord help me not give up so easily and stop short of the finish line. Replenish me so I can continue to run my race and operate in the purpose you have given me. Renew my strength so that I can do this again. Thank You Jesus for Your power today. Amen

Empty Vessels

Living for Jesus brings new perspectives to those around us, helping them see the love of Christ in action. If you squeeze an orange, orange juice comes out. If you pour water into an empty container and someone happens to tip the container over, the water you put in it is going to spill out, right? This is equivalent to your life. What's inside you will eventually come out. Nothing can come out of you that is not already inside you. Let's take it a step further. If you have rage and anger in you, it will eventually manifest itself in some way, shape or form. It's inevitable. If your heart is filled with bitterness and resentment, you restrict the Holy Spirit from pouring into your heart. When you're filled with evil, it is impossible to glorify God. You must offer yourself to God as an empty vessel to receive His spiritual blessing on your life. If you want to experience the fullness of God, you need to detox your mind, body and soul to create room for the Holy Spirit to fill you up.

2 Corinthians 4:8 We are pressed on every side by troubles, but we are not crushed. We are perplexed, but not driven to despair.

. . . .

. . . .

. . . .

. . . .

. . . .

. . . .

. . . .

Prayer:

Lord, sometimes I don't believe in my own abilities and skills. Help me see myself the way you see me each and every day. In Jesus' name. Amen.

Make it Happen

Overthinking is like a stationary bike. It's a lot of work without progressing forward. Healthy bodies are good but healthy souls are even better. In a culture where pace is quickened and being on a daily grind is expected, it's easy to try to orchestrate things to make them move at the pace and even in the timing you want it to move. Throughout my business career I have been blessed with many great opportunities while having multiple doors close. There was a time that I wanted a job so bad that I prepared for it, had mock interviews, met with others doing the role, met with mentors and coaches. I went and tried to orchestrate and say the right things, but it wasn't authentic. I was not being me. Unfortunately, I didn't get the opportunity I prepared so hard for. Sometimes, you can't make it happen on your own ability but when you do, it's because God has given you favor and strength. Yielding to the Holy Spirit, asking for guidance and direction. Remaining humble during the process regardless of the outcome. The truth is, life doesn't always go according to our plan. We'll have moments where everything is seemingly perfect, and all of a sudden it will catastrophically fall apart. We'll fall in love with the one we think is our forever and then we'll watch helplessly as the relationship crumbles. We'll pursue the career we hoped and prayed for and soon discover it doesn't make sense. We'll rise and then we'll fall but in time, we'll rise again.

Psalm 119:2 Blessed are those who keep his testimonies, who seek him with their whole heart.

Proverbs 23:17 Let not your heart envy sinners but continue in the fear of the Lord all the day.

Day

12

. . . .

. . . .

. . . .

. . . .

. . . .

. . . .

. . . .

Prayer:

Lord, open my heart and allow me to listen to Your daily prompts by faith and prayer. You are faithful and are always near the weary and confused. Thank You for Your mercy and grace in Jesus' name, Amen.

Praise Him in the Hallway

How often do we feel stuck in the "in between"? In between life seasons. In between jobs. In between relationships. In between goals. In between decisions. Sometimes the "in between" seems like it lasts forever. The real hard truth is that I'm still working through the in between. We all are under construction working through something. But here lies the truth for many of us, we cannot control when and how, and we will receive God's blessing. Now, I'm speaking from the perspective of a Christ follower and a born-again believer. Friends I've learned over the years the hard way that if you're a person that does well with structure and control then hanging out in the waiting room or hallway can sometimes be unbearable and will probably create a mini panic attack for you. But you have to know while you're waiting, God is working. Allow Him to take the reins and guide you to choosing the right door. The waiting process allows busy minded people to process, pray and seek God's direction and guidance on choosing the next door or opportunity. But friends, if you're going to be in the waiting room, why not breakout in praise and worship. When one door closes, just praise him in the hallway because you know by faith, God will open another one soon.

Revelation 3:20 Behold, I stand at the door and knock. If anyone hears my voice and opens the door, I will come in to him and eat with him, and he with me.

Philippians 4:6 Do not be anxious about anything, but in every situation, by prayer and petition, with thanksgiving, present your requests to God.

Day

13

. . . .

. . . .

. . . .

. . . .

. . . .

. . . .

. . . .

Prayer:

Lord help me not be anxious for anything but give me energy to seek You in prayer. Help me continue to be thankful for the open and closed doors because You are guiding and leading me for Your own good will. Allow me to be patient during the waiting process as it is strengthening my faith and perseverance. Thank You Holy Spirit for being with me in the hallway. Amen

It's Bigger Than You

Repeat after me, "We serve a big God and He can do big things!" Now as Ludacris would say, "Move chick, get out the way! Get out the way!" If you can do it by yourself then you really don't need God. Many times, God wants to do it so you won't have any doubt that it was Him and Him alone. If you're like me, I pretty much like to have some kind of control on how my day goes. Control in what is going on in my house and at work on my job, even if it's organized chaos. But there are some things that you can't control. You can't orchestrate simply because you are not the conductor. It is easier to trust God in the good times, but it takes faith to keep that trust during painful trials and tests. Tough times happen to everyone. It is sometimes difficult to believe that God is willing to take you through the impossible situations in your life. But we must put our faith over fear. In Matthew 9:29, two blind men asked Jesus to heal them. Jesus replied, "According to your faith will it be done to you" and their sight was restored. A ruler came and asked Jesus to put His hand on his daughter so that she might live. Because of the ruler's faith, Jesus brought his daughter back to life. The only thing you can control is your response, and the best response is activating your faith.

Matthew 9:29 Then he touched their eyes and said, "Because of your faith, it will happen."

. . . .

. . . .

. . . .

. . . .

. . . .

. . . .

. . . .

Prayer:

Lord give me the strength and the confidence to put my full trust in You. In the good times and the bad times. Help me not grow weary and depleted during times of uncertainty. Allow me to be a beacon of light to those in darkness because Your Holy Spirit is within me. In Jesus' name, Amen.

No, Not Yet

Sometimes your most applicable response, if asked about your progress is, "I'm not there, yet." That doesn't mean it won't happen. It just hasn't happened yet. I believe every closed door is a "not yet." Every missed opportunity is a "not yet," every loss or setback is an opportunity for a "not yet" moment. What's yours will come. The right people, the resources, the opportunities, the jobs, the passions, the hope. All these will find you when the timing is right. Exactly when you're meant to have it. When God knows you're prepared for it, you don't have to fight for it. You don't have to rush it. You don't have to live in a constant state of stress or anxiousness. Let go and let God. It's just not your time "yet."

Exodus 33:14 And he said, my presence shall go with you and I will give you rest.

. . . .

. . . .

. . . .

. . . .

. . . .

. . . .

. . . .

Prayer:

Lord as I seek Your presence, I ask You to move on my behalf and direct me during the times when I'm at my lowest moments in the valley. I believe I have everything I need while waiting on You. Hide me underneath Your wings. I won't be anxious, but I will continue to pray without ceasing. Amen

DAY 16
Failing Forward

Many times, we place expectations on ourselves of what we could've, would've, and should've done for God if we really had our act together. Failing is difficult but failing forward simply means you are still moving ahead and not remaining still or stagnant. What that means is that there is always a lesson to be learned and failure is one of our greatest teachers. When you make a mistake or fall short of a goal, you haven't failed if you've learned something from it. The faster and harder you fail, the less afraid you become because you have come out on the other side of it stronger and better equipped. Stay in the moment enough to learn from your failures and keep moving forward.

Psalm 73:26 My flesh and my heart may fail, but God is the strength of my heart and my portion forever.

Proverbs 24:16 For the righteous falls seven times and rises again, but the wicked stumble in times of calamity.

. . . .

. . . .

. . . .

. . . .

. . . .

. . . .

. . . .

Prayer:

God help me bounce back from my setbacks and build the confidence I need to overcome my fear of failure. In Jesus' name, Amen

DAY 17
Catch and Release

Have you ever tried to take every negative thought captive through basic discipline? The scripture tells us that when we take our thoughts captive, we can receive power to slay strongholds and extinguish our stinking thinking. What incredible power is available to us every moment of every day through the Holy Spirit! The more you release things that shut you down, the more freely you'll be able to give and receive God's limitless love. Fear will shut your heart, anxiety will shut your heart, judgment will shut your heart, resentment will shut your heart and the list goes on and on, but know this beloved, grace, peace, faith and love will create an opening. So, try to catch all that is good and start releasing all that is holding you back.

Proverbs 4:23 Guard your heart above all else, for it determines the course of your life.

John 14:18 No, I will not abandon you as orphans—I will come to you.

. . . .

. . . .

. . . .

. . . .

. . . .

. . . .

. . . .

Prayer:

Father, I set my mind on the things of the Spirit. I set my mind on your peace. I pray to grow more and more into the mind of Christ! Amen.

Disappointed But Not Defeated

Have you ever wanted something so bad that you think about it obsessively? I remembered just recently I applied for a new position at my job. I did all the research, prepared for the interview and was told there were other candidates who were more competitive, and it appeared my interview responses were canned. I was devastated because I felt like this job was perfect for me and it aligned with my aspirations and how I saw myself professionally in my career. It taught me a valuable lesson. We may be disappointed, but don't have to be defeated. God's promise is victory in Him. It might not come in the way we plan, dream, or hope, but He sees the bigger picture and we're right in the center of it. God's plan is bigger than ours. In our finite brains that's hard to grasp, but once we do, it changes our way of thinking. Disappointments are not meant to destroy us. We are not defined by our worst or our best. We are defined by our God.

Jeremiah 29:11 For I know the plans I have for you," says the Lord. "They are plans for good and not for disaster, to give you a future and a hope."

Romans 8:28 And we know that God causes everything to work together for the good of those who love God and are called according to His purpose for them.

Day 18

. . . .

. . . .

. . . .

. . . .

. . . .

. . . .

. . . .

Prayer:

Lord, help me accept disappointments and setbacks in stride, to allow them to strengthen me and make me better. In Jesus' name Amen.

Against the Ropes

Got mountains? Roadblocks? Hurdles? Obstacles? If so, I recommend being still for a moment and listen to that quiet small voice. Some people call it their inner voice, but I call it the Holy Spirit. Raise your level of discernment today. Some setbacks are just a setup for something greater. Life is 5% what happens and 95% how you react. Maybe you think it's broken, damaged goods, valueless or even hopeless. Well my dear friends let me tell you the greatest story is a comeback story. Counted out, but the underdog came back. Just like the late great Muhammad Ali, when he was up against the ropes boxing George Foreman. From the blows he was taking, you just knew he was done. It was blow after blow but then eventually George Foreman began getting tired, that's when Ali went or the kill. You might be in a "rope a dope moment" but God is in the business of turning beauty from ashes. You are not out of this fight and you are not fighting alone.

Ecclesiastes 4:12 And though a man might prevail against one who is alone, two will withstand him a threefold cord is not quickly broken.

Matthew 6:10 Your kingdom come, your will be done, on earth as it is in heaven.

....

....

....

....

....

....

....

Prayer:

God thank You for Your mercy and Your grace during all of my setbacks, beatdowns and breaking points. Thank You for preparing for my greatest comeback and breakthrough. I will not stay defeated. I'm ready Lord! Amen

Hallelujahs

Life is not a sprint, it's a marathon. The ones who thrive possess the agility to navigate the windiest roads and twisty turns. When I think about the many times when it would have just been easy to quit, it would have been easy to throw in the towel, but something told me that I have a Hallelujah break-through that is coming so keep moving and praising God. Now I'm not going to give you the impression that it was fast and I didn't regress but I can honestly say, Hallelujah I'm still moving forward because moving and making progress is more important than remaining stagnant. Here's the important part, when you want to give up and you get weary, God will not give up on you; it's just not in His DNA. So, what does never giving up really mean? It means believing in yourself. It means having a willingness to accept failure so you can learn and grow. It means not compromising on your most important values and walking the walk rather than just talking the talk. Hallelujah is the highest praise. So, can I get an Amen, and a Hallelujah because you have stayed the course and you just finished Day 20!

Exodus 15:13: In your unfailing love you will lead the people you have redeemed. In your strength you will guide them to your holy dwelling.

Isaiah 40:8 The grass withers and the flowers fade, but the word of our God stands forever."

. . . .

. . . .

. . . .

. . . .

. . . .

. . . .

. . . .

Prayer

God, give me a tenacious spirit and the mindset to grow and accept the things I cannot change but stay focused on the things that You can change. In Jesus' name, Amen.

Your Center Matters

My favorite part of an Oreo is the cream in the middle. Ok, I know there are haters out there that like the entire cookie sandwich, but the Oreo is known for the cream in the middle. And if you've ever had a double stuff or mega stuff Oreo then you know exactly what I mean. What's inside of the Oreo matters. I have met some really beautiful people on the outside that were horrible on the inside because of their terrible attitude, poor character, their entitlement, selfish mindset and hardened heart. Some people may not be very attractive on the outside, but on the inside, they are loving, compassionate, wise, gentle and kind, which is the way God wants us to be. The reality is that while beauty may be a reflection of what we see on the outside, our outside appearance is a direct reflection of how well we have taken care of the inside. God uses people no matter what they look like outwardly. The outside may be pretty but it's what's on the inside that counts. That means we should spend more time trying to be a good person than worrying about how good we look.

1 Samuel 16: 7 Man looks at the outward appearance, but the Lord looks at the heart.

1 Peter 3:3-4 Your beauty should not come from outward adornment, such as braided hair and the wearing of gold jewelry and fine clothes. Instead, it should be that of your inner self, the unfading beauty of a gentle and quiet spirit, which is of great worth in God's sight.

· ·

· ·

· ·

· ·

· ·

· ·

· ·

Prayer:

God when You look at me You see my heart and what's on the inside. Help me to see my beauty on the inside and be satisfied with how You created me. Amen

You Got This!

Are you underestimating yourself? Are you feeling like throwing in the towel? Most of us feel like this when people are against you and you don't have anyone who believes you can accomplish anything? Or maybe you came from broken dreams, a broken home or you're currently in a broken relationship. Maybe you had a complete breakdown and hit rock bottom only to realize that it doesn't matter what you say to yourself or what others say to you, you have to know, you need to love you! Speak to them dry bones and live. God said live! You are more than qualified and capable, beloved. It's time to shine, friend. Why can't it be your time? You prepared, you studied, you repositioned yourself, you refocused, and you prayed night and day, so let God be your steppingstone and allow me to give you a friendly Holy Spirit inspired nudge and push. You got this because God's got you!

Isaiah 58:11 The Lord will guide you continually, giving you water when you are dry and restoring your strength. You will be like a well-watered garden, like an ever-flowing spring.

Matthew 11:28 Then Jesus said, "Come to me, all of you who are weary and carry heavy burdens, and I will give you rest.

Day
22

. . . .

. . . .

. . . .

. . . .

. . . .

. . . .

. . . .

Prayer:

Lord, you are omnipresent, so as we conquer this day whether it's in the courtroom, boardroom, class-room, family room, or the ballroom, we need Your power today to conquer what we have in front of us. By faith, we are ready to win! Amen.

The Best Me

Stop whatever you're doing right now, go look at yourself in the mirror and repeat after me: " I am the best ME in the whole wide world." Ok that was good, but this time say it with conviction: " I am the best ME in the whole wide world." If you're a reflection of God's glory, when people meet you, they should meet Jesus. The person who you want to become will always be a moving target. You will always be a work in progress. Marianne Williamson said, "Playing small does not serve the world." There is nothing enlightened about shrinking, so that other people will not feel insecure around you. We are all meant to shine, as God's children do. It is not just in some of us, it is in every one of us. As we let our light shine, we unconsciously give others permission to do the same. As we are liberated from our fears, our presence automatically liberates others. It's simple, and sometimes too practical, but here it is—- Be an original not an imposter. Why be a cheap copy when God made you an original? Be the best you because everyone else is taken!

Romans 8:28 And we know that God causes everything to work together for the good of those who love God and are called according to his purpose for them.

2 Timothy 1:7 For God has not given us a spirit of fear and timidity, but of power, love, and self-discipline.

Day

23

· ·

· ·

· ·

· ·

· ·

· ·

· ·

Prayer:

Lord, it's hard sometimes not to worry about what others might say or think, so I ask You to help me be an original and become the best me each and every day. Help me to trust and have faith in you. Amen!

Choose Your Words Wisely

Our words have power and can create new doors and even close old ones. Your words can lead you down a pathway that you are not ready or prepared for. I admit, I have a tendency to worry about anything that I can't control. I've realized that I'm not the best presenter if I'm not passionate about it and you want me to speak on something without a structure. Give me an outline any day and I will be succinct, on point and probably even impactful. But if I don't have notes or structure I will ramble, run on and be all over the place when speaking. What we say has the ability to change the trajectory of those around us including ourselves. Words are more powerful than you can imagine, so it is important to choose them wisely. Unfortunately, our words can also lead us to places we wish we had never visited. So, let's try this together, first speak kind and nice words over yourself, like "you are enough, you have tremendous potential, you are needed, you are valuable." Start paying attention to that inner voice that might be criticizing and sabotaging you after making these positive affirmations. What is that voice saying? When you find yourself using negative self-talk, stop yourself, turn the words around and find the positive in the situation or experience. Learn to use empowering self-talk. If you change your words, you can change your life.

2 Timothy 2:16 Stay away from foolish, useless talk, because that will lead people further away from God.

Psalm 19:14 May these words of my mouth and this meditation of my heart be pleasing in your sight, LORD, my Rock and my Redeemer.

. . . .

. . . .

. . . .

. . . .

. . . .

. . . .

. . . .

Prayer:

Father, thank You for giving me emotions to express feelings and words to articulate Your goodness. Help me not use self-defeating words but allow me to replace them with kind words that will be like medicine to my soul and mental health. You are a healer and the restorer of all things. Help me get rid of my stinking thinking, in Jesus' name, Amen.

You Can!

I want you to know that your story is not over yet. This moment is the very cornerstone on which your story of faith will be built on. Beloved, one day you will soar. You will not be shaken by the turbulence because greater is He that is in you than he that is in the world. Beautiful moments of blessing and breakthroughs are waiting for you just ahead. Just know that if you have fallen, you will rise again. If you have seen darkness, the light is coming through. If you have faced failure or loss, you will recover a hundredfold by faith. If you feel lost, don't worry, make the right turn to Jesus and you'll be back on your path. And remember don't let anyone take you back to the place you prayed yourself out of!

Deuteronomy 20:4 For the Lord your God is he who goes with you to fight for you against your enemies, to give you the victory.

Exodus 15:2 The Lord is my strength and my song, and he has become my salvation; this is my God, and I will praise him, my father's God, and I will exalt him.

Day 25

. . . .

. . . .

. . . .

. . . .

. . . .

. . . .

. . . .

Prayer:

Lord I know I can do all things through you because you give me strength. Please give me the courage to do so. In Jesus' name, Amen.

Slow Your Roll

In this day and age, it seems everyone is trying to cram everything and anything into things that don't expand. I do it too while constantly feeling the pressure to pack my life full of activity and maximize my time by doing all I can do without even doing it.

In school, we're encouraged to join as many clubs, sport leagues, social organizations as possible to make the most of our social and educational experience. At work, it's expected that we'll be crazy productive and take on more and more responsibility to show that we have capacity because that's what is recognized. Even at home, there's a never-ending to-do list of things that need maintained, fixed or upgraded. Ughhhhh!

Even as I write this, I'm wondering why we do this to ourselves all the time. We must stop this quantity over quality thought process. We tend to squeeze so many things into one experience which creates a system overload that for me, equates to anxiety. Over time this is literally killing us slowly from the inside out. So why not just slow your pace for a little while and remain still enough to hear from God. Slow down, stop and yield to the Holy Spirit.

Jeremiah 2:25 Slow down. Take a deep breath. What's the hurry?

Psalm 46:10 Be still, and know that I am God: I will be exalted among the heathen, I will be exalted in the earth.

Day

26

· ·

· ·

· ·

· ·

· ·

· ·

· ·

Prayer:

Lord, slow my roll. Help me enjoy the moment and the opportunities that are provided each and every day. Help me be satisfied in You. In Jesus' name, Amen.

It's Only Over When You Quit

Your biggest enemy is YOU! When was the last time you did something for the first time and remained engaged in the process of doing it until you accomplished the goal? What's important is that you must keep fighting for what is good and right. Fight for your marriage, fight for your kids, fight for new opportunities, fight for your health. DON'T GIVE UP! You are not alone. You are in the hands of God. He will provide you with strength when you need it. One of the things you need to remember is that God is God in the good times and in the bad times. Whether you're on top of the mountain or in the deepest valley, God is with you. As God spoke to Joshua, He also says to you today: "Be strong and of good courage, do not fear nor be afraid...for the Lord your God, He is the One who goes with you. He will not leave you nor forsake you" (Deuteronomy 31:6). You see, success doesn't come from the absence of problems; it comes from the presence of the One who goes through them with you! Will you quit or will you press through? The choice is yours.

Isaiah 40:29-31 He gives strength to the weary and increases the power of the weak. Even youths grow tired and weary, and young men stumble and fall; but those who hope in the Lord will renew their strength. They will soar on wings like eagles; they will run and not grow weary; they will walk and not be faint.

Day

27

. . . .

. . . .

. . . .

. . . .

. . . .

. . . .

. . . .

Prayer:

God, You are faithful and true. You stick with me during the good times and the bad times. You are with us when we win and when we lose. Thank you for Your presence in my life. Amen.

Keep the Pace, The Walls Will Fall

Slow progress is still progress. My husband always says, "A slow grind is better than no grind." Either move toward building your empire or become another girl who could have, should have, would have built one. It's so easy to feel defeated when you have been praying, fasting and believing God for something and nothing ever changes. You start journaling, watching videos, listening to podcasts only to have zero results. The Bible has a very clear answer for that feeling of defeat: Don't quit! That's right – don't quit when things get tough in your life. Did you know that even Jesus Christ Himself wanted to quit on the way to the cross (Luke 22:42), but He didn't. Thank God. Many times, people give up just short of achieving their dreams. If they had endured just a little longer, victory and triumph would have been theirs. Nothing worth gaining comes without sacrifice.

This reminds me of the story about the Israelites' faith to walk around Jericho until they experienced their victory. The wall of Jericho was destroyed when the Israelites walked around it seven days carrying the Ark of the Covenant. On the seventh day, Joshua commanded his people to walk around the wall seven times then blow their trumpets made of rams horns and shout until the wall finally fell down. This story tells us that you can have a lot of faith but if you don't have action you won't get results. The combination is the key. Not all works, not all faith but faith and works are the right combination to conquer those walls. Remember God's plan is not always our plan, but His plan is the right plan. While your plan for the perfect life is ideal, God's plan for your life is incredible. Jeremiah 29:11 says, "For I know the plans I have for you," declares The Lord, plans to prosper you and not to harm you, plans to give you hope and a future." Don't lose faith beloved, God still has a divine and full tested plan for you and me.

Romans 15:4 For everything that was written in the past was written to teach us, so that through the endurance taught in the Scriptures and the encouragement they provide we might have hope.

James 1:3 Because you know that the testing of your faith produces perseverance.

Day

28

. . . .

. . . .

. . . .

. . . .

. . . .

. . . .

. . . .

Prayer:

Father help us not try to be God and take the steering wheel of our lives but help us yield our lives back to you so you can take Your rightful place in our lives. Lord help us not grow weary when our walls don't instantly fall but give us perseverance to press through. In Jesus' name, Amen.

DAY 29
Plan J— "Jesus"

Stop asking people where you're going or how to get there when they've never been there themselves. Sometimes we can't sense God's presence because there's too much of everything else going on around us. Too much noise. Too much traffic. Too much confusion. Too many thoughts running rampant in our minds. Too much anxiety. Too much fear. Too many voices. Center your mind on Him and take a deep breath. Try it. Exhale the distracting thoughts. Inhale peace, tranquility, calmness and mindfulness. Exhale your focus on self. Inhale a desire to know Him more completely. Exhale the worries of the moment. Inhale His peace. Now, don't you feel better already? Just imagine Him embracing you and like my kids would tell us when they were little, I want a squeeze hug. Can you sense that you're safe in His arms? There's a reason His word says, "Be still and know that I am God." Your Plan J (Jesus) is the best strategic plan you can implement to regain your peace. His plan will always be better than yours, because He knows the end from the beginning. You only know the past and the present. Woosah, He's ready to give you the best squeeze hug ever.

Philippians 4:19 And this same God who takes care of me will supply all your needs from his glorious riches, which have been given to us in Christ Jesus.

Psalms 91:11 For He will give His angels charge concerning you, To guard you in all your ways.

. . . .

. . . .

. . . .

. . . .

. . . .

. . . .

. . . .

Prayer:

Lord we don't need a plan B when we align our desires, passions and wants with You. Father, help us rest and focus on the bigger vision and plan You have for lives. Help us yield our will to Yours. In Jesus' name, Amen.

DAY 30
Create Space for New Beginnings

Every breath you take is a new beginning. Living intentionally in the present takes discipline. Have you ever stopped and wondered why some people seem to receive more than you do even when you did the same things they did to receive it? Could it be that they have actually made room and decluttered their mindset and repositioned their thinking? I believe God wants the best for us but if you never made room or cleared out some things, you will never experience the full magnitude of something new and exciting. I recall when I was setting up my office space at work. My wall art and pictures were hung nicely in place, but I left about a 11x14 space on the wall. For many who would come by my office they would notice the awkward open space on my wall. That was my act of faith. I was working on this designation for several years. Two to be exact. I just needed a reminder to continue to press through, but it also served as a placeholder for my designation. See there is liberation and freedom when you remove things that weigh you down or don't belong. There is a feeling of exhilaration when we lighten our loads, plan for the future and reposition ourselves for something new. Get ready for the new thing God is about to do in your life.

2 Corinthians 5:17 Therefore, if anyone is in Christ, the new creation has come: The old has gone, the new is here!

Job 8:7 Your beginnings will seem humble, so prosperous will your future be.

. . . .

. . . .

. . . .

. . . .

. . . .

. . . .

. . . .

Prayer:

Yahweh, correct my attitude, mindset and behavior and reposition me to receive what You have in store for me. Create a new beginning and a restart. Give me a steadfast spirit. In your name I pray, Amen.

A Shot of Vitamin "C"

Vitamin C is an essential vitamin. That means your body can't produce it. Vitamin C plays many roles and has been linked to impressive health benefits. Vitamin C is an essential need for the human body just as Christ is to a believer. "Likewise, the Spirit also helps in our weaknesses. For we do not know what we should pray for as we ought, but the Spirit Himself makes intercession for us with groanings which cannot be uttered." Romans 8:26. What do you do when faced with the unknown? Do you give in to panic? Or do you buckle down and trust what you know to be true about God? Trusting God is like taking a shot of vitamin C (Christ).

Acts 3:6 But Peter said, "I don't have any silver or gold for you. But I'll give you what I have. In the name of Jesus Christ the Nazarene, get up and walk!"

. . . .

. . . .

. . . .

. . . .

. . . .

. . . .

. . . .

Prayer:

Jesus, You are great, and You are worthy to be praised. I thank you for giving me renewed strength and Christlike mindset. Help me not only grow in my faith but be a reflection of You. In Jesus' name, Amen.

We All Get Weary

God hears you even when you can't find the words to say anything. Depression is not a sign of weakness, it's a sign that you're human. We all experience emotions whether you're anxious, depressed, defeated, fearful, bitter, resentful, suspicious, or even apathetic. Everybody has bad days. Poor mental health negatively affects how we think, feel, and act. It also helps determine how we handle stress, how we relate to others, and helps us make healthy choices. Although people often interchange, poor mental health and mental illness are not the same thing. A person can experience poor mental health and not be diagnosed with a mental illness. Likewise, a person diagnosed with a mental illness can experience periods of physical, mental, and social well-being. The name of the Lord is a strong tower and in Him we are safe. You are not down and out, you're just sad and it is ok to feel sadness. Give yourself a little grace but seek the help you need. We were not created for isolation but for community.

. . . .

. . . .

. . . .

. . . .

. . . .

. . . .

. . . .

Prayer:

Lord, I can't do life without depending on You. In You I live and move and have my being. I can't stand firm unless I'm standing on the Rock that is higher than I. Thank You for being my rock and firm foundation. Amen

Just Say "No"

Here's a fun fact: Hurting people hurt people. I know that doesn't sound deep or profound but it's true. Unhappy people like to unload their problems and concerns on others. It's their M.O. (Modus Operandi or mode of operation). When people use others as their emotional garbage disposal with no desire for feedback or healing, it's toxic and unfair. Remember, you are the gatekeeper to your life and your emotional well-being. You don't have to give people an all-access pass. Sometimes it's necessary to remove yourself from the situation and regroup. Saying "yes" to something automatically means saying "no" to something else. When I think about it, each twist and turn of my life's journey has meant sacrificing one thing for something else. I want to let you know that it's okay to say no. In fact, "no" can be the greatest blessing you could ever give yourself and others.

Psalm 37:4 Take delight in the LORD, and he will give you the desires of your heart.

. . . .

. . . .

. . . .

. . . .

. . . .

. . . .

. . . .

Prayer:

Lord, Your mercy and grace endure forever. Thank You for keeping my mind and emotions from break-down and allowing me to breakthrough. Thank You for Your love that never fails. You are the vine and I'm staying connected to You. Amen

Get Out of the Boat

You're familiar with the story of Peter walking on the water with Jesus while they were in the midst of a storm, aren't you? Even as a child this story intrigued me and as a full-grown adult, I am still in awe of the fact that Peter defied the laws of gravity to do the impossible. Although it was only for a moment, Peter did what the other disciples dared not do; believe Jesus for the impossible. Sometimes it takes crazy faith to get crazy results. Once you take your eyes off of Jesus who is the author and finisher of our faith, you open yourself up for fear, doubt and worry to set in which will cause you to miss out on your miracle. Keep your eyes on God's plan and He will cause you to go places you never dreamed you would go.

Matthew 14:28 "Lord, if it's you," Peter replied, "tell me to come to you on the water."

Day

34

. . . .

. . . .

. . . .

. . . .

. . . .

. . . .

. . . .

Prayer:

Lord, give me the strength and faith to trust You even when chaos is all around me. Surround me with people who help encourage me to seek You and to grow closer to You. When I can't seem to shake worry and fear, allow me to remember Your promise that You have not given me the spirit of fear but of power, love and a sound mind. Amen

You're Not Broken, You're Becoming

Have you ever spent a considerable amount of money on the latest gadget or electronic device only to get it home, open it up and realize it doesn't work as advertised? Just ask my husband about the surround lights he bought online twice. Not really what he expected. LOL! For many of us, the first thing we do is open up the user manual to troubleshoot the issue so that we can get the full benefits of the product we purchased. Just like we refer back to the owner's manual when our electronic devices or any other product we own isn't working, we need to refer back to God's word when our lives are in disarray and out of order. When we are at our weakest, God is our strength. When we are at our lowest, God gives us hope to rise again.

Psalms 119:105 "Your word is a lamp for my feet and a light on my path."

. . . .

. . . .

. . . .

. . . .

. . . .

. . . .

. . . .

Prayer:

Lord when I feel like I'm broken and nothing in my life seems to be working, open up my eyes to see clearly that Your word is all I need to get an understanding of what Your will is for my life. Mend the broken areas of my life and make me whole again. Amen

DAY 36

My husband always tells me that when I smile, I show every tooth in my mouth. I'm not sure that's even possible. He often tells me when you laugh you go all in and it's contagious. There is nothing that works faster in order to bring back the mind and body into balance than a good laugh. Sometimes we can take ourselves too seriously and forget to enjoy the stretching process along the way. Now we know with growth it's not always comfortable or pain free but it's a necessary process and hopefully progress towards what you have been aiming for. Laughter is said to release special hormones that help with stress, anxiety and worry. Think about it, you can't feel anxious, angry or sad when you're laughing. Some things are just not funny and honestly some things are inappropriate to laugh at, like funerals.... but there are moments you have to laugh because you know what you're doing is not working and if we could hear the audible voice of God He probably would say, "are you done yet?" So, brighten up a little with a little giggle. It will make you and those around you feel better.

Genesis 21:6 Sarah then said, "God has given me cause to laugh, and all who hear of it will laugh with me.

. . . .

. . . .

. . . .

. . . .

. . . .

. . . .

. . . .

Prayer:

Lord help me feel the presence and Your joy during my times of disappointment and allow my mind to set towards the beauty of laughter. In Jesus name, Amen.

Just Watch

It's not always easy to believe in yourself, especially when the odds seem to be stacked against you. But believing in yourself, even when others don't, is one of the most powerful forms of self-love there is. If you spend every hour and minute seeking validation from others, you will miss out on the opportunities that could create tremendous growth. Learning how to believe in yourself with unstoppable, unshakable faith is a skill. Here's the good news, you can cultivate and develop this skill. So, what does it really mean to believe in yourself? Ultimately, it means coming in agreement with God's belief in you. That's true freedom. Freedom from worry and unrealistic standards that insignificant people put on you. Freedom to grow and become who God called you to be. Freedom to be purpose-driven and growth-centric. Freedom to be YOU; the whole you.

1 John 4:4 But you belong to God, my dear children. You have already won a victory over those people, because the Spirit who lives in you is greater than the spirit who lives in the world.

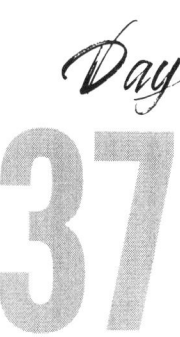

Day

37

. . . .

. . . .

. . . .

. . . .

. . . .

. . . .

. . . .

Prayer:

Lord, help me to believe and put my full trust in You. Lead me through the wilderness and help me be confident in my present and hopeful about my future. In Jesus' name, Amen.

The "Glow Up"

The "glow up" is real. Have you ever gone back to a high school class reunion and saw the high school nerd who transformed into the successful businessperson, the bullied, often teased and picked on is now the big executive of a Fortune 500 company? How you start doesn't always dictate how you will finish. Many people want and expect instant results without sacrifice or changing habits or behaviors. You have a choice in where you focus your energy. Life is about choices. You have the choice to settle for less or go for more. You are not subject to your behaviors, genes, or circumstances. Instant results are just that; instant. When you focus all of your energy on the outcome, you will forget about the daily sacrifices it took to get where you need to be.

Psalm 51:10 Create in me a pure heart, O God, and renew a steadfast spirit within me.

2 Corinthians 5:17 Therefore, if anyone is in Christ, the new creation has come: The old has gone, the new is here!

. . . .

. . . .

. . . .

. . . .

. . . .

. . . .

. . . .

Prayer:

Father, teach me to be patient during my process of transformation. Allow me to accept that true transformation takes sacrifice and hard work. I pray for restoration in Jesus' name, Amen.

Love Yourself First

Women are naturally caregivers and usually have a tendency of being everyone's everything while leaving the scraps for themselves. I will be the first to admit this is an area of growth opportunity for me. Being a wife, mother, boss lady and even a dog mom, everyone's needs are usually met before mine. In the event of an emergency on a passenger airplane, you have to put your oxygen mask on first before putting the mask on those who depend on you. If you try to help others first, you won't be any good if you pass out due to a lack of oxygen. Loving yourself first means taking care of the whole person spiritually, physically and mentally first before pouring into the lives of others. You love yourself by treating yourself with respect, care and concern. Now don't get me wrong, this doesn't mean be so consumed with yourself exclusively but loving yourself enough to forgive yourself and give yourself permission to be loved. Remember your identity is found in Christ.

1 Corinthians 25:10 By the grace of God, I am what I am.

· ·

· ·

· ·

· ·

· ·

· ·

· ·

Prayer:

God, give me the confidence to love myself first and to share my love for others freely without a judgmental heart and mind.

God I surrender myself to You. Sometimes I feel like my needs and desires are forgotten by others. I get weary in doing good. Rejuvenate me and help me love myself enough to set boundaries and respect myself enough to not settle for less. In Jesus' name, Amen.

DAY 40
Hiccups

Has your life been a series of hiccups? Mine sure has. Hiccups are so annoying. No matter how many sips of water you sip it doesn't make them instantly go away. Sometimes you're told to hold your breath and try to count to ten, but they still hit ya with an unexpected jerk. Unexpected events happen all the time like a random series of the hiccups. One thing is for certain and that is we will experience hiccups that bring failure, disappointment, uncertainty and broken trust. It's all part of this journey we call life but if you're a child of God, it's the wilderness moments that produce tremendous spiritual growth. Sometimes God will use the wilderness to wean us off our own self-centeredness, self-reliance and self-righteousness so that we can realize that our sufficiency is in Him alone. If you feel like you're in the wilderness right now, don't be discouraged, just hold your breath because the wilderness is only for a moment. Like an occasional series of hiccups, God is bringing you out and you will come out of it stronger, wiser and better.

Matthew 4:1 Then Jesus was led by the Spirit into the wilderness to be tempted by the devil.

. . . .

. . . .

. . . .

. . . .

. . . .

. . . .

. . . .

Prayer:

God, You knew my end from the beginning and although I feel like I'm in the wilderness, I believe You will lead me to my land of promise and prosperity in You. Thank You for walking with me in my wilderness. I praise You in advance because You are leading me to my destiny in You. In Jesus' name, Amen.

This is How I Fight My Battles

Most of our battles in life take place on the battlefield within our minds. Life is like school, filled with many lessons to be learned during each stage of our growth. Those of us that learn our lessons are fortunate enough to move onto the next stage, while others are left to repeat the class. For me it was freshman college Zoology 101 class, it was my nemesis. Having a defeated mindset is the wrong position to be in when going into a battle. The battle usually starts in your mind because of the way we think. Sometimes perceptions are not the true reality. If we regularly think about good things, godly thoughts become natural. Countless thoughts flow through our minds every day but we have the choice to stay in a negative space or believe for the best. We may feel we have no control, but we do. Although we don't have to use any effort to think wrong thoughts, it takes much effort to think good thoughts. So, don't let the enemy count you out because you were made to win. You have a well-equipped army of angels on your side. Let your enemies know, they don't want none of this!

Deuteronomy 30:19 "I call heaven and earth to record this day against you, that I have set before you life and death, blessing and cursing: therefore, choose life, that both thou and thy seed may live:"

· ·

· ·

· ·

· ·

· ·

· ·

· ·

Prayer:

Almighty God, help me to monitor my thoughts, choosing only those thoughts that will help me overcome the devil and win the battle for my mind. In Jesus' name I pray. Amen.

Make Room

Is your life jammed so packed with junk and your own agendas that there is no room left for God? Maybe you're like me, the person that says, "here God, you can have the top small zipper compartment of the roller suitcase." Every time we go on an extended weekend trip and it involves flying, my suitcase is usually the one flagged by the airline because it is over the limit by five pounds or more. We then have to either remove items, put on items or just pay for the over limit fee. It's easy to fit God in especially when it's on your own terms but that's not what He does for you and I.

Girlfriend, it is time to declutter our lives to allow the Holy Spirit to have space to freely move. God delights in being with His people. He wants to be close and live within us. But He leaves it up to us to declutter our life to make room for Him in our hearts. We need to prioritize time to meet with God, share life with Him and discover how to become who He intended us to be. God wants full access to the full suitcase, not just the small compartment that can only fit a toothbrush or a comb. He deserves an all-access pass to your heart.

Matthew 18:12 If a man has a hundred sheep and one of them wanders away, what will he do? Won't he leave the ninety-nine others on the hills and go out to search for the one that is lost?

. . . .

. . . .

. . . .

. . . .

. . . .

. . . .

. . . .

Prayer:

Lord, help me make You the number one priority in my life. You have full and unlimited access. Thank You for never leaving me or forsaking me. Amen.

The Real You

The masquerade party is over and it's time for the reveal. We often wear masks to hide or to portray a certain image that we deem is acceptable by societal norms. I believe that being authentic is key to living a satisfying and meaningful life. Being authentic is being your true self, with honesty, openness and transparency. Sometimes we can be constrained by our own perception of what authenticity is. I've learned if we have to continually suppress who we really are, and hide what we think, believe and feel, it's a recipe for illness, depression, and failure. No one can be you and you can't be someone that you're not, that would be so exhausting. But people do it every day especially when they have a need to be accepted by others. Here's the good news, God accepts you the way you are, flaws and all. So, don't worry about getting the approval from everyone else. You were made in God's image and God doesn't make mistakes.

Colossians 3:17 And whatever you do, in word or deed, do everything in the name of the Lord Jesus, giving thanks to God the Father through Him.

. . . .

. . . .

. . . .

. . . .

. . . .

. . . .

. . . .

DAY 44
Crush Negative Thoughts

I said to myself, "Enough is Enough. You may have lost that battle, but you will not lose the entire war!" If no one is cheering for you then it's time to get some pom poms, start your own dance squad, or drumline and get a whistle and say, "Ready (pause) OK!" Stop focusing on your defeats, past failures, & shortcomings, and begin focusing on your wins; big or small. You don't need anyone to validate who you are.

Friends, I've learned something in my pursuit of a stress-free life: If I want peace rather than stress, I must choose to seek direction from God in every situation and not rely on what I want to happen but what God allows to happen. He will always lead us toward peace and joy, not anxiety and frustration. In fact, it is in your pain that God is closest to you, whether you realize it or not. The Bible says in Psalm 34:18, "The Lord is close to the brokenhearted and saves those who are crushed in spirit."

Psalms 34:18 The LORD is near to the brokenhearted and saves the crushed in spirit.

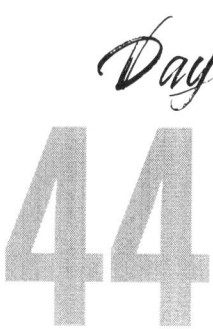
. . . .

. . . .

. . . .

. . . .

. . . .

. . . .

. . . .

Prayer:

Father, I release my negative and destructive thinking and I ask for Your help to allow me to speak words of life to myself and others. Help me see myself how You see me through Your son, Jesus Christ. Allow me to walk with boldness and confidence with humility and strength. I release it all into Your hands in Jesus' name, Amen.

DAY 45
Dancing in The Rain

Have you ever just stopped and started praising God for His mercy and grace? I think it's time to have a "dancing in the rain" moment. There is no limit to how, when, or where we can praise God. But I've found sometimes you have to confuse the hard-hearted people by being kind, confuse the selfish people by being a giver, confuse the negative people by showing positivity and confuse the gloom and doom with rays of hope. Now I'm not saying you should act oblivious of your circumstances, that's careless but what I am saying is praise your way through your circumstances and lean on God's word. Whisper a prayer to God throughout the day. So, when you're driving down the road in your car say, "God, thank You for allowing me to have a safe drive." Or, when you're hanging out with friends, whisper, "God, thank You for surrounding me with a community that cares about me." When you're going through a difficult season say "God, thank you for teaching me and leading me through this." Praising God in every circumstance gives us joy and it pleases God. God gets glory from every act of praise no matter what shape or form it comes in.

Matthew 6:33 But seek first His kingdom and His righteousness, and all these things will be given to you as well.

Day

45

. . . .

. . . .

. . . .

. . . .

. . . .

. . . .

. . . .

Prayer:

God, I thank you for being a just and on time God. Nothing that happens to me in vain. Your will is purposeful. Give me the boldness and confidence I need to praise and worship through my current situation and circumstances. In Jesus' name, Amen.

Know Your Why

Are you aware that God has a purpose for you? That your true identity is not what you put on your resume. It's not determined by your zip code or by the type of the car you drive. Most people struggle with three basic issues in life. The first is identity: "Who am I?" The second is: "Does what I do matter?" And thirdly is: "What is my purpose?" Over the past decade, I have struggled in this area and it wasn't until last year when I found my why. Many people think your purpose has to be grand or complex but really, it's usually something simple that you can understand and hopefully articulate. God has a wonderful plan for your life to bring about good. It is important to realize that plan. If you don't yet know what God has for you to do, ask Him to reveal it to you. Ask Him for a vision for your life.

Psalms 37:4 Trust in the LORD and do good; dwell in the land and enjoy safe pasture. Delight yourself in the LORD and He will give you the desires of your heart. For evil men will be cut off, but those who hope in the LORD will inherit the land.

Philippians 1:6 And I am certain that God, who began the good work within you, will continue His work until it is finally finished on the day when Christ Jesus returns.

Day

46

. . . .

. . . .

. . . .

. . . .

. . . .

. . . .

. . . .

Prayer:

Lord, reveal to me my purpose and what You have called me to do so I can live intentional with no regrets. Amen

Bitter Root

The flower will last as long as the root system supports it. Bitterness occurs when we feel someone has taken something from us that we are powerless to get back. It is impossible to leave the past behind and get on with your life while you are living with unforgiveness. It causes bitterness and resentment, which overflows into your present day. Bitterness is like experiencing a very slow death that ultimately destroys your peace of mind. Forgiveness does not mean pretending everything is Ok. It doesn't mean forgetting the hurt either. According to St. Augustine, forgiveness is simply the act of surrendering our desire for revenge; that is, our desire to hurt someone for having hurt us. Forgiveness is the gift we give ourselves that enables us to stop picking at the scab and start making a plan to have a release party to celebrate our healing. When you are offended or disappointed by others and allow the hurt to germinate in your heart, bitterness and resentment will take root. Get to the root issue, pull up the weed from the root and then figure out how it got there and what you need to do to keep it from coming back. Everything is a process, that includes your healing.

Hebrews 12:14-15 Make every effort to live in peace with all men and to be holy; without holiness no one will see the Lord. See to it that no one misses the grace of God and that no bitter root grows up to cause trouble and defile many".

Day

47

. . . .

. . . .

. . . .

. . . .

. . . .

. . . .

. . . .

Prayer:

Lord, heal us from the areas no one ever apologized for. Free us from bitterness so it does not grow into resentment, in Jesus' name, Amen.

When Your Efforts Seem Fruitless

When you do everything for everyone, you pray and fast and still don't get a breakthrough. Kids are still out of control, emotions are unbalanced, failing on your job, the only thing left is to release and discover the truth that the Lord's mercies are new every morning (Lamentations 3:21-23). I learned to abide in that grace instead of walking in my guilt and failures, accepting His mercy in my inadequacies. Gradually, peace replaced my desperation and God revealed His heart to me as He refined the fruits of mercy and forgiveness in my life.

Lamentations 3:22–24 The steadfast love of the LORD never ceases; his mercies never come to an end; they are new every morning; great is your faithfulness. "The LORD is my portion," says my soul, "therefore I will hope in him."

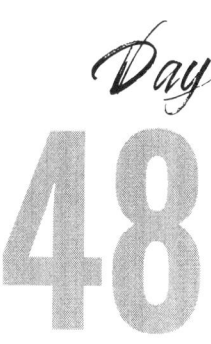

. . . .

. . . .

. . . .

. . . .

. . . .

. . . .

. . . .

Prayer:

Lord, help me to seek Your peace and put away my destructive thoughts. Allow me to accept Your grace and to show grace to others. In Jesus' name, Amen.

Concentrate on His Word

You never know how empty or thirsty you are until you have an encounter with God. Just like the woman at the well, we don't know how thirsty we are until we find ourselves in His presence. Dwell for a while in God's presence. All of the promises and everything in God's word are for you, but you have to be conscious of them. Spend time in His word. You have to renew your mind daily so you can be aware of all of His precious promises. It's not a matter of God's faithfulness, it's a matter of your faithfulness to Him and His word. It's time to get focused on God's word.

I Corinthians 14:33: For God is not the author of confusion but of peace.

Psalms 46:10 Be still and know that I am God.

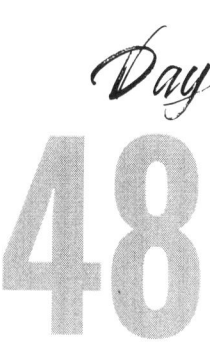
. . . .

. . . .

. . . .

. . . .

. . . .

. . . .

. . . .

Prayer:

God Your word is true, and I will lean on its principles each and every day. Please give me the focus, endurance and obedience to lean on Your word. Remove all the distractions that will keep me from fulfilling the purpose You have outlined for my life. In Jesus' name, Amen.

Cherish the Moment

No matter what time it is, it is always now. Nothing ordinary is meant for you. Living in the present does not mean surrendering our responsibility to correct some things from the past or to plan and make way for the future. In fact, it is the ultimate taking of responsibility for both. The truth is, there is only now. Only God knows the past, present and future. You can only live in this moment right now. That's why you need to make this moment count. What's happened in the past has passed and what is going to happen depends on what you do right now. Make every moment matter and cherish it.

Proverbs 27:1 Do not boast about tomorrow, for you do not know what a day may bring.

Psalms 118:24 This is the day the LORD has made; let us rejoice and be glad in it.

. . . .

. . . .

. . . .

. . . .

. . . .

. . . .

. . . .

Prayer:

Lord, thank You for giving me breath in my lungs, a beating heart and for allowing me a new opportunity to seize the day. I cherish every God given opportunity You provide for me. Amen

DAY 51
Semicolons (;)

A semicolon is a punctuation mark indicating a pause, typically between two main points, that is more pronounced than that indicated by a comma. When I was 16, I was driving down the road. As I approached a four-way stop, a large truck ran through the stop sign and t-boned me. My car spun out of control upon impact. Luckily, I had on my seatbelt and wasn't ejected from the vehicle. The accident was so bad that first responders had to use the jaws of life to cut me out of the car. I was rushed to the hospital. Miraculously, I had only suffered from a few scratches. Nothing broken, bruised or damaged. That was my first semicolon moment. In professional writing, a semicolon is used when an author could've ended their sentence but chose not to. It represents continuance. You are the author and the sentence is your life and you're choosing to continue. It would be easy for you to check out and throw in the towel. Honestly there is so much a human being can take. My second semicolon moment was when I found out I was pregnant with our first child. It was during my junior year in college. I was not married, and I felt like my life was ending. I was young, afraid and clueless. What the enemy intended for a period; God created a divine semicolon. I got married, obtained my bachelor's degree and even persevered to receive my master's degree. The pause was just the beginning. This book would never end if I continue to share all of my semicolon moments, but the premise is this, you may be experiencing something that may feel like an end or like a period. But those are moments when you cry out to God and ask him for grace and mercy. Remember, God always wins in the end.

2 Timothy 1:7 For the Spirit God gave us does not make us timid, but gives us power, love and self-discipline

. . . .

. . . .

. . . .

. . . .

. . . .

. . . .

. . . .

Prayer:

Lord I thank You for being my strong tower during the storms of life. There are so many times it could have been a period, but it was a semicolon. Which means You gave me another chance. Thank You for the courage and the confidence to overcome anxiety. There is power in those semicolon moments. Amen

Debits and Credits

There is power in your words. When someone truly believes in you and shows you that they do, it gives you an extra lift on your wings. When you need that extra push, it can help you to soar a little higher and fly a little faster. There are so many people in my life that have either added to my value or made a deduction from my worth. No one can make you feel small or useless unless you allow them. We must agree that words of affirmation can make you feel like you chugged a can of Red Bull and now you have wings. When people don't believe in you or speak opposition, it's as if they are debiting from your account. The reason people refuse to believe in you is because they don't see what you see. They don't have the vision you have for your life. But at the end of the day, if you're not sowing seeds (credits) into your life by positive self-talk and actions, you will remain in a deficit. Sometimes the best thing you can do is believe in yourself and invest in your own dreams.

Colossians 3:17 And whatever you do, in word or deed, do everything in the name of the Lord Jesus, giving thanks to God the Father through him."

. . . .

. . . .

. . . .

. . . .

. . . .

. . . .

. . . .

Prayer:

Dear God, remind me of the simple truth that confidence can only be found in chasing after You. Help me walk with boldness and proclaim that I am enough, I am loved, and You have rescued me. Help me not use self-hate and self-doubt as distractions to living out my purpose. Father, please bring people into my life that add credits not debits spiritually, mentally and emotionally. In Jesus' name, Amen.

Extra in the Ordinary

Most of the time life is very mundane and ordinary. We get up, get ready for our day, go to work, do our job, come home, go to bed and then do the same thing all over again the next day. But why continue and do the same thing every single day? Switch it up a little and do something out of the ordinary so you can experience extraordinary results. Extraordinary starts with you. Doing a little "extra" with ordinary things, skills, behaviors, by just adding a little drop of faith on it and following your faith with action. Most of the time there are small opportunities we all have encountered but we got comfortable and played it safe. But remember friend, God has extraordinary, special moments and opportunities for you in the midst of your ordinary life and daily routine.

Job 8:7 Your beginnings will seem humble, so prosperous will your future be.

Day

53

· ·

· ·

· ·

· ·

· ·

· ·

· ·

Prayer:

God, work through me and equip me with everything I need to accomplish immeasurably more than all I ask or imagine. Take my ideas to the extreme. Push the envelope of creativity within me. Help me exceed my expectations in every area of my life through Your power alone. In Jesus' name, Amen.

Teachable Moments

There are teachable moments all around us. History has proven that if you don't learn from it, you will be doomed to repeat it. Time and experience can be excellent teachers when you actually learn a lesson from your poor decisions. Past regrets can steal your joy and happiness and derail you from focusing on what is good. There is nothing wrong with failing if you learn from it. As a parent, there are times when you see it crystal clear that your children are heading down a path of destruction and you let them know, but they still want to make their own decisions. In those moments, you have to allow them to experience the consequences of their choices so they can learn from them. It's easy to constantly keep a safety net below your children so if they fall you can keep them from hitting the ground. However, if you continue to be that safety net, they will never learn how to recover through the process. Sometimes you just have to let your child fail. As parents we do our children a disservice when we protect them from natural consequences when we take over for our kids to ensure they don't fail. Believe me, as long as it is not going to be detrimental to your child or lead them to sin, give them room to fail. Sometimes this is the best gift you could ever give them.

Proverbs 3:6 in all your ways submit to him, and he will make your paths straight

Psalm 37:23 The LORD directs the steps of the godly. He delights in every detail of their lives.

Day

54

. . . .

. . . .

. . . .

. . . .

. . . .

. . . .

. . . .

Prayer:

Lord, enlighten my mind so that I could better comprehend that all good things take time. Bless me with Your guidance and direction each day of my life. Remind me that patience is an essential trait of a good Christian. Help me learn from my failures and learn through the teaching process. In Jesus' name, Amen.

Sticks and Stones

People might not physically hurt you, but their words can destroy your self-confidence if you allow them to. You've heard the phrase "Sticks and stones may break my bones, but words can never hurt me." That statement is so far from the truth. That mindset may help us keep a resilient will and a stiff upper lip, but we know from experience it's not true, especially when it comes to our heart. Words are powerful and can create lasting imprints or memories. We've all been wounded at some point by careless, unkind or downright mean things that were said to us. Their effect on our lives, even years later, is undeniable. I remember when I first started my professional career working for a large corporation. I was eager, driven and ready to conquer the world. I knew early on that I had a desire for leadership and that I could operate at the next level, but I had a supervisor with a different opinion. She was terribly critical and never provided any support or words of encouragement. We all will encounter people that don't believe in you and some will be bold enough to tell you that you're not valuable. You have to learn that even if they don't believe in you, you must believe in yourself. Sometimes it's necessary to find a support system by casting your net wider and finding people that can help you grow and who truly believe in you and help push you. As for my supervisor, the funny thing is I ended up being her boss. So even though she didn't see me at the next level, God promoted me two levels more. No matter what tough exterior we try to put on, words can really influence the way you think about yourself. They have the power to build up and the power to tear down, but we must be careful and choose the words we say. Learn to speak life to others instead of tearing their life down by your words. Your words matter.

Ephesians 4:29 Let no corrupt word proceed out of your mouth, but what is good for necessary edification, that it may impart grace to the hearers.

Proverbs 18:21 Death and life are in the power of the tongue, and those who love it will eat its fruit"

Day
55

· ·

· ·

· ·

· ·

· ·

· ·

· ·

Prayer:

Lord, help me speak life-giving words and not words of destruction. In Jesus' name, Amen.

Meant For More

We were made for more! More than our failures, more than the vicious cycles of defeat, more than being ruled by our habits, our body image, social media and our guilty pleasures. We were made to overcome and conquer. God's plan for our lives is for us to be whole, lacking nothing in Him. He built us to need Him. God has more for us than our addictions, insecurities, low self-esteem and lack of confidence. If you still have air in your lungs, there is more for you to do on this earth. Here's the truth, you were not created to merely survive in this life. No! You were made to create, strive, achieve, learn, lead and be a witness. You were created to bring glory to God with your everyday life! You have unspeakable value and I know that for a fact!

Esther 4:14 For if you remain silent at this time, relief and deliverance for the Jews will arise from another place, but you and your father's family will perish. And who knows but that you have come to your royal position for such a time as this?

Day
56

. . . .

. . . .

. . . .

. . . .

. . . .

. . . .

. . . .

Prayer:

Father God, we praise You for who You are. You are a mighty God. You are a faithful God. You are the Lord who calls us by name. You promise to hold our hand so we don't have to walk alone. You've redeemed us. You've put Your Spirit in us that we may enjoy freedom from captivity and the lies of the enemy. I was made for a purpose and made for more, I will walk with boldness today. Amen.

A Little Favor, a Lot of Faith

I never understood why some people seemed to get all the breaks and have more success than others. Either the difficult situation becomes easy or the complex situation is now simplified. I used to think that my husband must have a "special" relationship with the trinity because he always seemed to have favor. Whether it was getting in free to the World Series baseball games, walking the red carpet at the Grammy's or getting front row tickets to multiple live concerts. It was about five years ago I point blank asked him, "What are you doing to catch all these breaks?" And he simply said, "When God is involved, it is just putting on the confidence of the Holy Spirit and walking in favor." I believe there is no such thing as luck. There is no cosmic force that lines up to make things work. Nothing happens by chance. The truth is it's all God. So, the next time you feel lucky, or you think you're on a streak of good luck, remember, it's not luck at all it's called favor. God's favor will take you places you would never dream of. God's favor is worth more than money. God's favor can open doors that degrees can't open.

Proverbs 16:33 says this, "The lot is cast into the lap, But its every decision is from the Lord."

Day

57

. . . .

. . . .

. . . .

. . . .

. . . .

. . . .

. . . .

Prayer:

Lord I have favor in You and rely on your goodness and mercies that are new each and every day. Lord help me to not covet after my neighbor's track record and focus on my own race in Jesus name, Amen.

Power of Choice

If the devil can't make you sin, he will make you busy. What you get out of life is in your control. What you value, what you believe in, what you do every day isn't determined by someone else. It doesn't matter what your parents, friends, family members tell you. You have the ability to control your destiny. Every day you are presented with choices to either respond, adjust, reject or adhere to. I recall when our son was in the sixth grade, he wanted to play the clarinet in the school band. He never played an instrument before, but he was set on playing the clarinet. The band director at the time would assign instruments and you were lucky if you got the instrument of your choice. Assignments were over and the band director called him into his office and said, "We have enough clarinet players, but I really need a saxophone player." He said it's considered a woodwind as well, but it takes a different skill that I believe you can master with practice. My son was hesitant because he had his mind set on playing the clarinet, but he really wanted to play in the band and decided he will try something different. Six years later, he is one of the top saxophone soloists in the band, a member of the high school jazz ensemble, and All Regional Player of the Year. He would have never accomplished any of that if he didn't make a God-led decision. He could have taken the defeated route and said, "never mind I don't want to play," but he took the risk and chose something different than expected. Some choices are critical, and some choices are just a test of your faith. Choose wisely and be open to trying something new. You're one decision away from the biggest opportunity in your life.

Isaiah 30:21 If you wander off the road to the right or the left, you will hear his voice behind you saying, "Here is the road. Follow it."

Psalm 119:105 Your word is a lamp to guide me and a light for my path.

. . . .

. . . .

. . . .

. . . .

. . . .

. . . .

. . . .

Prayer:

God, remind me that my thoughts are not Your thoughts and my ways are not Your ways when I am struggling to see clearly and making decisions. Lead me and guide me so that I can be in Your will. In Jesus' name, Amen.

Mentor-Sista-Friends

Life is not meant to be experienced alone or without community. We were created to have relationships with others. When you reach the end of your life, you'll no doubt look back and remember the people who mattered and the memories you made with them. I thank God for the ladies he has sent in my life along the way to help me enjoy the journey. I call them "Mentor-Sista-Friends." A "mentorsistafriend" is someone who is more than a sister or even a biological relative. They are individuals who come to our defense, wipe away our tears, take care of us when we are sick, encourage us in bad times, and support our goals and dreams. At the very same time, these same women would not hesitate to correct you, scold you, push you, even anger you or challenge you in order to get the best out of you. They truly want the best for you and believe in your future. The sad reality is, many women despite their achievements or power are too afraid, too selfish, or too insecure to help other women. So even if you're not receiving this type of support, I encourage you to be that support and encouragement for someone else.

Proverbs 18:24 There are "friends" who destroy each other, but a real friend sticks closer than a brother.

Ruth 1:16 But Ruth replied, "Don't ask me to leave you and turn back. Wherever you go, I will go; wherever you live, I will live. Your people will be my people, and your God will be my God.

. . . .

. . . .

. . . .

. . . .

. . . .

. . . .

. . . .

Prayer:

Heavenly Father, lead me to love and mentor others in a way that grows them in Your love. In Jesus' name, Amen.

DAY 60
Praise Break

Life is a series of peaks, valleys, highs, lows, tests and trials. How you respond will determine your destiny or demise. Have you ever done something so radical in your life that left everyone around you dumbfounded, confused and in awe? When your back is against the wall or when you're overcome with anxiety, worry or fear, I dare you to do the unthinkable and give God a praise in the midst of your trouble and watch what God does in response. The bible tells us that "God inhabits the praises of His people." *Psalms 22:3* Sometimes it's not a matter of getting out of your situation, it's letting God get the situation out of you. Praise is the key that unlocks the door to your freedom in the spirit realm. Although it may seem like you're in an earthly prison, your praise is the way to break out of it. Hallelujah!

Acts 16:25-26 But about midnight Paul and Silas were praying and singing hymns of praise to God, and the prisoners were listening to them. And suddenly there came a great earthquake, so that the foundations of the prison house were shaken and immediately all the doors were opened, and everyone's chains were unfastened.

. . . .

. . . .

. . . .

. . . .

. . . .

. . . .

. . . .

Prayer:

Lord there is no greater place to be than in Your presence. Sometimes I feel bound by chains and shackled by the cares of this world, but I lift up a praise to You in the midst of my mess because You dwell in the midst of my praise. Thank you Jesus! Amen

Glass Half Empty or Half Full

Two construction workers walk into a diner during their lunch break. After working outside in the scorching heat, they both sit down at the booth and the waiter brings them both a glass of ice water filled halfway. One of the workers slams his fist on the table and demands more water. The other worker expresses his gratitude for the cold drink. Which of the two workers do you identify with? In life we don't always get what we want but whatever we do get, we must learn to appreciate it. The glass half empty and glass half full argument has been one disputed for generations and will most likely be disputed for many generations to come. What I've learned in my life here on earth is that when we shift our attention from what's in the glass and express gratitude for the mere fact that God has given us a glass, we learn to be more appreciative. We are simply vessels of the most High being used for His glory. Sometimes we feel empty and depleted while other times we feel full of joy and happiness. Whether we are empty or full, we must realize we are His workmanship and should be ready and willing to be used for His glory.

Philippians 4:11 "...for I have learned to be content whatever the circumstances."

. . . .

. . . .

. . . .

. . . .

. . . .

. . . .

. . . .

Prayer:

Heavenly Father, I thank You that You choose to use me in the midst of my flaws and shortcomings. I count it an honor and privilege to serve You and to be a light to those in darkness. Whether I am empty or full, I am Yours. Use me for Your glory. In Jesus' name, Amen.

Your Test = Testimony

It would surprise you if you knew how many people live vicariously through other people's lives and through other people's walk with God. It's one thing to proclaim you're a believer but it's another to have battle scars to prove you're a true soldier in the army of the Lord. It's not enough to proclaim you're a Christian by wearing a trendy t-shirt, WWJD bracelet or a spiritual bumper sticker on your vehicle. When you give your life to Christ there will be a testing of your faith and the devil is eager to bring attacks in your life to make you waver in your walk with God. You may have been an alcoholic, drug addict, lived a promiscuous lifestyle or battled with pornography in your past. Whatever the case may be, when Jesus saves you from that old sinful nature, you are given a license to testify about the saving grace of God to others who are lost. Your testimony is a weapon that can quench the fiery attacks of the enemy and give God glory for saving your soul. Whenever God opens a door of opportunity to share your testimony with others, don't hesitate to take advantage of it. You may be the fresh breath of hope they need to give their life to Christ. Your test is your testimony.

Revelation 12:11 And they overcame him by the blood of the Lamb, and by the word of their testimony; and they loved not their lives unto the death.

. . . .

. . . .

. . . .

. . . .

. . . .

. . . .

. . . .

Prayer:

God, You are almighty and have all power. There is nothing too hard for You. Thank You for every test and trial. Thank You for every setback and every time You brought me out of the storms of life. Give me the courage to share my testimony with others so that they may come to know you more. In Jesus' name. Amen

DAY 63
Standing Ovations

I take compliments with a grain of salt. Although they're nice to hear, I don't take them for granted. But I've also learned if you only perform for the applause of others then you place your happiness in the hands of your audience. Don't get me wrong, it feels good when people acknowledge something good about me and it's very humbling but one thing you must understand is the same people that cried "Hosanna, Hosanna" to Jesus were the same ones who said crucify Him a few days later. When people who are from the same place you come from see God moving mightily in your life, they tend to remind you of your past or your upbringing to discredit the great work God is doing in you. This is a sad reality, but you must keep your eyes fixed on Jesus who is the author and finisher of our faith. If not, you will easily get discouraged and give up. When people applaud you, thank them and give all glory to God and keep it moving. Don't get so caught up in the ovations of man that you lose sight of God's plan and purpose for your life.

Mark 6:4 But Jesus said unto them, "A prophet is not without honor, but in his own country and among his own kin and in his own house."

Day

63

. . . .

. . . .

. . . .

. . . .

. . . .

. . . .

. . . .

Prayer:

Lord thank You for every gift and talent You've given me. Even for the gifts that have not manifested yet. Be glorified in my life and teach me to not be so attached to the accolades and ovations of others but to seek validation and approval from You. Remove any pride or self-centeredness that may be lingering in my life and keep me humble. In Jesus' name. Amen

Lessons & Lifeboats

In every storm we encounter in life there's a lesson. Every life experience has a teachable moment. Every difficulty is for your development. In fact, everything we go through is an opportunity to grow and learn. Think back on all of the things you went through, good and bad. How many of those things caused you to be wiser, stronger and better? Oftentimes God saves us from things that would have taken us out. These are what I consider lifeboats. Think about it. There are times when it seems like everything around you is about to be destroyed but God extends His grace and saves you from it. We are surrounded by troubled waters and raging seas disguised as worry, depression, sin, anxiety, temptation and more but all we have to do is channel our faith in Jesus to calm the seas of life and reassure us that we will reach our destination because He is in control.

Matthew 8:26-27 Jesus replied, "You of little faith, why are you so afraid?" Then He got up and rebuked the winds and the waves and it was completely calm. The men were amazed and asked, "What kind of man is this? Even the winds and the waves obey Him!"

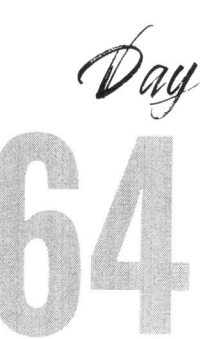
· ·

· ·

· ·

· ·

· ·

· ·

· ·

Prayer:

God, the storms I'm facing seem overwhelming. I am afraid, worried and in despair. I need reassurance that everything will be alright because You have the power to calm the storms and You can give me peace in the midst of it. I surrender to Your will and I put my trust in You. In Jesus' name, Amen.

Through the Fire

The bible is filled with stories and miracles that absolutely blows my mind. People being raised from the dead, God speaking through a donkey, water coming from a rock, and so many more. One story that resonates with me is the story of three Hebrew boys named Shadrach, Meshach and Abednego that refused to bow down to worship idols of gold. When King Nebuchadnezzar heard they refused to comply with his orders, he ordered them to be thrown into a fiery furnace. Although the king intensified the heat seven times hotter, Shadrach, Meshach and Abednego told the king that even if he throws them into the fire, they trust that Almighty God will deliver them and even if God didn't deliver them, they were not bowing down to any idol gods. When they were thrown into the fire, they went in as a three-man unit but when the king looked closer, He could see a fourth person in the furnace with them. Once the king realized they were not being consumed by the fire, he called them to come out of it. When they came out, not one single hair on them was burned, not even their clothes smelled like smoke. Here's the part where I shouted! When we are going through what seems to be our hardest trial and test or when we are facing persecution, we are not alone. God never said we wouldn't have to go through trouble in this life, but He promised He would never leave us nor forsake us. Don't be afraid when the fire comes because when you're in the will of God, He will be with you through the fire. Hallelujah!

Daniel 3:27 So Shadrach, Meshach and Abednego came out of the fire and the satraps, prefects, governors and royal advisers crowded around them. They saw that the fire had not harmed their bodies, nor was a hair of their heads singed; their robes were not scorched, and there was no smell of fire on them.

. . . .

. . . .

. . . .

. . . .

. . . .

. . . .

. . . .

Prayer:

God, Your word says You will never leave us nor forsake us. Sometimes I get discouraged and feel like I'm fighting this battle alone. The evil in this world is overwhelming but in the midst of it all, I refuse to allow the enemy to reign in my life. I submit to your will for my life and my family. We trust you to deliver us from all evil. In Jesus' name. Amen

Mountain-Mover

Do you have any mountains in your life? Are you facing something that seems impossible? When things look impossible to our human eyes, remember that we have God Almighty, the Mighty Mountain-Mover on our side. Oftentimes we make a mountain out of a molehill by our perceptions of a problem. There are times when I tend to focus on things that take me off course. You cannot worry and worship at the same time. When we surrender our troubles to God, we are actually acknowledging the truth that we're not adequate enough to meet the demands of life in our own strength. God is everywhere at all times. There is no place, no matter how alone we may feel, that God cannot be. He is everywhere! Jesus said "For assuredly, I say to you, whoever says to this mountain, 'Be removed and be cast into the sea,' and does not doubt in his heart, but believe that those things he says will be done, he will have whatever he says." Be a mountain-mover now and beyond! Be a mountain-mover on the authority of God's Word given to you through Jesus Christ and the revelation of the Holy Spirit! He will not fail you.

Mark 11:23-24 Therefore I say to you, 'Whatever things you ask when you pray, believe that you receive them, and you will have them.

. . . .

. . . .

. . . .

. . . .

. . . .

. . . .

. . . .

Prayer:

Father, there are obstacles in my life and those around me that I can't seem to overcome. I need You. I need Your mighty power. Please fill me with mountain moving faith in Jesus Name.

DAY 67
Lost & Found

Have you ever lost something and frantically searched for it only to discover you had it with you all along? I had a favorite pair of earrings that were so cute. They were cheap but I absolutely loved them. I lost them almost nine months prior and finally discovered them in a hidden pocket in a purse that I hardly ever used. I compare that pair of earrings to the hidden gifts and talents we have within that we never utilize because of fear, doubt or worry of criticism from others. Our gifts and talents were not meant for us to hide but to be used for God's glory. People hide their talents because they might not know what to do with them. Some hide them because they don't know how to use them, so they give excuses as to why they didn't use them. Some of us might not use our gift because we are insecure and feel that they're not good enough. Just think about it, if everyone hid their talents, then how would anything be created? There would be no art, books, medicine, electricity, computers, technology, etc. I can go on and on. Don't let your gift and talent go to waste. There are many talented people in the grave who never gave birth to their dreams. Stop searching for something that you already have.

James 1:17 Every good and perfect gift is from above, coming down from the Father of the heavenly lights, who does not change like shifting shadows.

· ·

· ·

· ·

· ·

· ·

· ·

· ·

Prayer:

Lord, I was lost, and You found me. Thank You for giving me gifts and talents. I will not be selfish. I will use them to glorify You in all that I do. Amen

Breaking Point

Everybody has a breaking point and sooner or later someone or something is going to push you to that breaking point. The way you respond to the breaking point will determine your demise or your destiny. I truly believe that life's setbacks only come to expose who you really are, the real you. And right when you least expect it, boom! Life will hit you with a blind-sided blow that knocks the wind out of you. For some, it may come while raising a child, for others it may be the stress from your finances and for many of us, it may be self-inflicted. Either way it comes, we all are going to experience a breaking point in our lives. So, let me encourage you to immediately run "to" God and not run "from" God when this happens. Let your breaking point be a making point that creates a tipping point into your purpose so you can live life with clarity and accuracy. God can use your breaking point as a turning point to experience His amazing grace and mercy.

Matthew 11:28 "Come to me, all you who are weary and burdened, and I will give you rest."

. . . .

. . . .

. . . .

. . . .

. . . .

. . . .

. . . .

Prayer:

Lord I'm in a state of emergency. I feel broken and at my wits end. I don't know what else to do and that is why I'm coming to You. I need You now more than ever. I am desperate for a touch from You. You know my situation and You know the fear and anxiety I have because of it. Right now, I cast all my cares on You because I know You care for me. Give me peace that surpasses all understanding so that I may walk in the path You set for me with confidence. In Jesus' name. Amen

Seize The Moment

Life is but a moment and by the time you know it, it's over. It seems the older I get, the quicker time flies by. I can't count how many times in my life when I feel like I missed opportunities because I was too distracted with things that really didn't matter. There is nothing more frustrating than looking back over your life and realizing how much time was wasted chasing your own agenda, pursuing the wrong career or even trying to cultivate the wrong relationships. Once I repented to God for my mismanagement of time and for drifting off the path He planned for me, I learned to seize every moment God ordained for me. The safest place in the whole world is in the will of God. If you still have breath in your lungs, you still have time to get back on track with God's plan for your life. Seize the moment.

Psalms 90:12 So teach us to number our days, that we may gain a heart of wisdom.

· ·

· ·

· ·

· ·

· ·

· ·

· ·

Prayer:

Father forgive me for wasting so much time and so many precious moments. I repent for mismanaging the days, weeks and hours given to me. And I ask that You give me the wisdom and discernment to maximize each moment I have to help fulfill Your purpose for my life and to help others reach their full God-given potential on this earth. In Jesus' name. Amen

DAY 70
His Grace is Sufficient

One of my favorite people in the Bible is Paul. Paul persecuted the church before he had a road to Damascus experience with God that changed the trajectory of his life forever. Paul wrote a majority of the books we read in the New Testament. He performed miracles under the power of the Holy spirit, he was well-educated and spoke several languages. Paul was a true man of God. But one thing that makes Paul so relatable is his transparency of the fact that just like all other human beings, he had weaknesses and battled with the flesh. When he sought the Lord regarding his shortcomings, God reminded him that His power is made perfect in Paul's weakness. In other words, wherever you may be lacking strength, wisdom or ability, God's grace is sufficient for you to make up the difference. God is the difference-maker and there is nothing too big that His grace can't handle.

Psalm 5:12 For you Lord, bless the righteous one; You surround him with favor like a shield.

2 Corinthians 12:9 But he said to me, "My *grace is sufficient* for you, for my power is made perfect in weakness."

Day

70

. . . .

. . . .

. . . .

. . . .

. . . .

. . . .

. . . .

Prayer:

Lord thank You for Your grace that is so amazing. I can't earn it or work for it. You so freely give it and I am thankful for it. Your grace is enough. Nothing else compares to it. In my weakness I can trust that Your strength is made perfect. I have power in You to overcome any test or trial that I face. Thank you Jesus. Amen

Just Turn the Page

It's imperative for you to know that you are not standing helplessly alone in your valley. God Almighty is with you and he is fighting for you. In fact, He's already taken on every Goliath in your life and has declared the victory. As you go through different stages of your life, God has promised to never leave you nor forsake you. As the days, months and years go by, just like reading a good novel, the story intensifies, and God is right there with you every step of the way turning the pages of your life. And just when you think the story is over, God allows a plot twist in the midst of your despair and the Holy Spirit revives you and gives you the courage to keep going. You are destined for greatness. Just keep on going because it gets greater later.

"My flesh and my heart may fail, But God is the strength of my heart and my portion forever."

. . . .

. . . .

. . . .

. . . .

. . . .

. . . .

. . . .

Prayer:

Lord it gets hard sometimes. Life throws me so many curve balls and I get to the point of giving up, but Your grace and mercy remind me of the hope that is in You. Help me to be reminded that even though there are plot twists in my life's journey, You have given me the victory in the end. In Jesus' name, Amen

Small Steps

They say a journey of a thousand miles begins with one step. That sounds good and very simplistic doesn't it? However, whenever we have our hearts and minds set on doing something significant, many of us have a tendency to lose patience and we get frustrated because we want it now. We live in a day and age where everything seems to be moving at warp speed. But if you've ever achieved any level of success in your life then you know the necessity of patience and perseverance. Our timing must align with God's timing and sometimes that requires us to take things one step at a time and one day at a time. We must learn to celebrate the small victories on our way to the big ones. But it's going to require obedience, discipline and patience. God never calls us to do something without equipping us. Small steps add up to big results and consistency creates new opportunities.

Psalms 37:23 The steps of a good man are ordered by the Lord, and He delights in his way.

Day

72

. . . .

. . . .

. . . .

. . . .

. . . .

. . . .

. . . .

Prayer:

Lord, Your plans for me are good but sometimes I get anxious and I want things to move at my pace and in my own timing. Teach me to slow down and enjoy the present and not be so consumed with the future. I put my time and my life in Your hands so that You can show me the value in waiting on You. Thank You for giving me the discipline to persevere. Amen

Giant Slayer

Imagine having all the odds stacked against you. You're unqualified. You don't have the educational background. You're not a part of the in crowd. You're not strong enough. There is absolutely no way you will come out of this victorious. But then you take a moment to look back over your life and you're reminded of all the battles God brought you through. How many times He caused you to triumph over what was supposed to take you out. And then you realize that it was never your own strength and abilities that brought you through it. It was God and God alone. That's when you have the courage like David to look your giants in the face and declare the victory because greater is He that is in you than he that is in the world. Giants come in all shapes and sizes. For David it was Goliath. For others it may be a giant of divorce, sickness, loneliness, fear or anxiety. Whatever giant you are facing, take confidence in knowing that your God is bigger than any circumstance you face, and He is well able to slay your giants for His glory!

1 Samuel 17:50 So David triumphed over the Philistine with a sling and a stone; without a sword in his hand he struck down the Philistine and killed him.

Day

73

. . . .

. . . .

. . . .

. . . .

. . . .

. . . .

. . . .

Prayer:

Lord, I put my trust in Your word. Give me the confidence to declare Your word over my situation and to walk in boldness. I am more than a conqueror in You, and I thank You that the battle is not mine but it belongs to You. In Jesus' name, Amen.

Better Days

Better days are faith-filled days. Faith is moving forward, familiar is going back. God expects us to keep moving and trusting Him in the forward movement. Gratitude is a word that holds a lot of power. All things are possible through those that believe. When you have a heart of gratitude, it encourages you to move forward. Finding peace and joy in the simple things in life doesn't depend on our ability to acquire as many things as we can, it requires us to be content in what we have. Finding contentment in the things that matter like your family, your faith, your well-being and your health. Better days come when you find joy and peace within and not allow others to define who you should be or how you should be. Better days are when you are fully authentic, transparent and honest with who you are; unapologetically.

Colossians 3:23 Whatever you do, work heartily, as for the Lord and not for men,

Day

74

. . . .

. . . .

. . . .

. . . .

. . . .

. . . .

. . . .

Prayer:

Lord thank You for Your grace and mercy and for Your comfort during my dark days because You are my shield and shelter. By faith I believe better days are coming in Jesus' name, Amen.

Are You Done?

Sista, are you done? Are you done trying to orchestrate your own plan instead of God's plan? Are you done trying to control others instead of controlling yourself? Are you done trying to be perfect in an imperfect world? Are you done trying to gain the approval of your boss and others? Are you done trying to climb the corporate ladder on your own? We can do everything in our power to make our days go as planned and still, somehow feel like we're falling just short of our expectations. Striving for our own definition of perfection, or someone else's, can leave you worn out, exhausted and very disappointed. Stop trying to orchestrate everything and have a little faith. Stepping out in faith sounds easy, but it means leaving your comfort zone and facing your fears head on. Today is a good day to stop relying on your own strength and start leaning on God's. God never asks us to figure it out on our own. He just asks us to trust Him, to recognize His leadership and sovereignty in our lives and He promises to make our pathways straight.

Psalm 32:8 I will instruct you and teach you in the way you should go; I will counsel you with my loving eye on you.

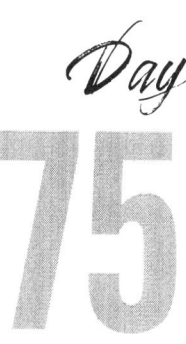
. . . .

. . . .

. . . .

. . . .

. . . .

. . . .

. . . .

Prayer:

Dear Lord, forgive me for seeking approval from everyone but You. Teach me to be silent so I can hear You. Thank You for loving me enough to help me grow. In Jesus' name, Amen.

DAY 76
Laser Focus

Many of us are not achieving goals or being successful in life not because we lack the mental or physical capacity to achieve them. Truth is, we already have everything we need in us to fulfill God's plan for our lives. What's missing is our lack of focus. It's easy to be distracted by so many different things on a daily basis. Whether it's a busy schedule full of tasks and events, social media, television, even friends and family members who drain us of all our energy and passion. When you are laser focused on your goals and minimize our distractions, you are unstoppable. What does it mean to be laser focused? Laser focus is intensely paying attention to a single object, concept, person or activity to the exclusion of everything else. When you set your eyes on the prize of the high calling of God on your life and make His plan a priority, He will ultimately give you the desires of your heart.

Philippians 3:14 I press toward the mark for the prize of the high calling of God in Christ Jesus.

. . . .

. . . .

. . . .

. . . .

. . . .

. . . .

. . . .

Prayer:

God, give me the desire to focus solely on Your purpose for my life. Remove any distractions or road-blocks that would come to hinder your plan for me and my destiny in You. In Jesus' name, Amen.

Promise Keepers

Webster's dictionary defines a promise as "a declaration that one will do or refrain from doing something specified." Every single day we make promises to our spouses, our children, our loved ones and even to ourselves that we often don't keep. I don't want to make light of broken promises because broken promises have significant repercussions. Marriages have been destroyed because of broken promises. Businesses have collapsed because of broken promises. Teenagers become rebellious because of broken promises. Regretfully, I have broken many promises that have caused a lot of hurt and disappointment. It is very difficult rebuilding trust once a promise is broken. When we learn to put our trust in Jesus (the one who has never broken a promise) and we allow the Holy Spirit to reveal our inability to do it on our own, we will learn to extend grace to others and also gain the nature of God to honor our word.

2 Corinthians 1:20 For all the promises of God in Him are yes, and in Him Amen, unto the glory of God by us.

· ·

· ·

· ·

· ·

· ·

· ·

· ·

Prayer:

God, You are a promise keeper. All of Your promises are true and trustworthy. Teach us to walk in integrity and to honor our word. Let our light shine to those in darkness that they may see You through our witness. In Jesus' name. Amen.

Be Flawsome

Calling all flawsome people! I'm flawsome, how about you? Friends, stop striving to be perfect. Embrace your flaws and imperfections. If you need to improve, start improving. If you need to change, start the process. If you want to grow, plant the seed and water it. What are you waiting on? Being flawsome is hearing that voice of fear in your head, but saying, "Okay, but the truth is, God made me on purpose and for a purpose." Flaws and all I am fearfully and wonderfully made. I am beautiful. When Jesus died, He left a part of himself for You and I. We are flawsome because the Holy Spirit dwells within us. We can be bold and courageous. When you and I embrace our flaws and let go of the idea of perfection, that begins the process of truly discovering who we really are. We no longer have to concern ourselves with who we think we should be.

Isaiah 61 1-3 The Spirit of the Lord God is upon me; because the Lord hath anointed me to preach good tidings unto the meek; he hath sent me to bind up the brokenhearted, to proclaim liberty to the captives, and the opening of the prison to them that are bound; To proclaim the acceptable year of the Lord, and the day of vengeance of our God; to comfort all that mourn; To appoint unto them that mourn in Zion, to give unto them beauty for ashes, the oil of joy for mourning, the garment of praise for the spirit of heaviness; that they might be called trees of righteousness, the planting of the Lord, that he might be glorified.

. . . .

. . . .

. . . .

. . . .

. . . .

. . . .

. . . .

Prayer:

Lord, I am determined to be the person You called me to be. I will embrace my flaws and shortcomings because I know Your grace is sufficient for me. Amen

Long Suffering

I ask God questions all the time. Sometimes it's as if I'm a little child walking around the house behind Daddy (God) asking lots of questions like "Why do good things happen to bad people?" Or "why do innocent children suffer from starvation and disease?" Many of the questions I often ask are biblical. Recently while I was reading God's word, I came across the word "longsuffering" and I couldn't help but question God what that meant. The revelation He gave me was powerful. Longsuffering is one of the characteristics of love. It is also one of the fruits of the Spirit. The word longsuffering means "suffering long." I know that's not deep or profound but it's just a summarized meaning. When we encounter major trials and tests in our lives whether that's the loss of a loved one, turmoil in our marriage or problems with our children, it's hardly ever a quick and easy process. It involves long suffering which in turn produces patience and perseverance. The next time you find yourself in a situation that looks like it's going to take you out, get in God's word and brace yourself for the ride because when it's all said and done, God is going to get every ounce of glory out of it He deserves.

1 Corinthians 13:4 Love suffers long and is kind.

. . . .

. . . .

. . . .

. . . .

. . . .

. . . .

. . . .

Prayer:

God, You work all things together for my good. The good things and the bad things. Sometimes it hurts but I know You will be glorified when it's all said and done. Help me in my times of doubt and despair so that I can come to a place of confidence and faith that You are in control. In Jesus' name. Amen

DAY 80
Bounce Back Kid

My husband grew up in a modest family where his mother had to struggle to make ends meet on a very low income, but she made it work. I remember him telling me that he was often laughed at in school because of his worn-down clothes and his shoes had holes in them. It hurt his feelings but deep down inside he sensed that God would not allow him to always be the poster child for hard times and lack. He continued to read God's word and pray daily. Fast forward to adulthood, God has blessed him over the years not just financially but also spiritually and it's funny that those same people back in the day that pointed their fingers and laughed at him are the same ones with their hands out asking for favors. I believe when you are a good steward over that which God entrusts you, He will bless you abundantly. If you're in a season where you can't seem to catch a break, hold on just a little while longer. Help is on the way. God is a rewarder of them that diligently seek Him.

Proverbs 8:17 I love those who love me, And those who seek me diligently will find me.

. . . .

. . . .

. . . .

. . . .

. . . .

. . . .

. . . .

Prayer:

Heavenly Father, thank You for Your provision and for Your protection. Although sometimes we experience lack and hardship in life, You always provide for Your children. Give us the wisdom and discipline to be good stewards over that which You've entrusted us and allow us to be a blessing to others. In Jesus' name. Amen

You Got This!

You got this because God's got you. Yes, I'm speaking to you, friend. You got this because you are greater than you think you are. If you're a child of the Most High God, then you're already winning! Stop apologizing and being so critical of yourself. When you are moving forward and making incremental progress, it's still progress. There comes a time you just need to look at yourself in the mirror and tell yourself, "I got this!" We may not all be equal in talent, but we should be equal in our effort. That's because God can do a lot with a little. So, lean all the way in, my friend and rely on His strength.

Colossians 1:11 Be filled with His mighty, glorious strength so that you can keep going no matter what happens, always full of the joy of the Lord.

Joshua 1:5 "No one will be able to stand against you as long as you live. For I will be with you as I was with Moses. I will not fail you or abandon you."

. . . .

. . . .

. . . .

. . . .

. . . .

. . . .

. . . .

Prayer:

Lord, thank You for being my Heavenly Father. Thank You for being a mighty God. Thank You for keeping me and guiding me. Amen

Prayer Closet

Are you looking for a way to become more committed and intentional with your prayer life? Have you ever wanted your very own secret space in your home to spend some quality time with God? One of the most essential rooms in my home is my prayer closet which is a walk-in closet in my master bedroom. Not only do we use my prayer closet for a place of refuge if there is a tornado. It is also used when I'm experiencing life's tornadoes. In the far back corner, I have carved out a small space to retreat, release my worries to God and pray. A prayer closet can be anywhere we are free to experience uninterrupted intimacy with God. So technically it could be in the bathroom, in your garage, your car or while sitting at your desk at work. Even if you have limited space, you can still take a few minutes out of your day to sit in solitude, listen to the Lord and call on His name.

Hebrews 12:11 No discipline seems pleasant at the time, but painful. Later on, however, it produces a harvest of righteousness and peace for those who have been trained by it.

Day

82

· ·

· ·

· ·

· ·

· ·

· ·

· ·

Prayer:

Lord help me to keep it simple and not complicate things with communicating with You. You are my hope when I feel hopeless, my strength in a time of weakness and joy when we I'm feeling grief and sorrow. You are always just a prayer away. Amen

Rinse, Spin and Repeat

Do you ever feel like you're caught in a cycle? Many people are just going through life just like that. Passing through. It's like dirty clothes going through the rinse cycle, non-stop rinse, spin and repeat. Letting time tick away. Just sitting there letting things happen. Watching every day be just like the day before and the day after that. Nothing out of the ordinary. Nothing different. Nothing unique. Just average. Many people are living their entire lives without ever standing up and stepping out. Most people stay in the same cycle because they fear failure, but it comes a day when you want it so bad that you will assume the risk of missing a step, jumping out in the deep end or changing directions. The cycle will stop when you stop grumbling and have a heart of gratitude and thanksgiving. It's time to change the setting so you can begin living life in a new direction.

2 Corinthians 5:17 Therefore if any man be in Christ, he is a new creature: old *things* are passed away; *behold*, *all things* are become new.

Day

83

. . . .

. . . .

. . . .

. . . .

. . . .

. . . .

. . . .

Prayer:

Heavenly Father, I am tired of going through the motions and not making progress. Release me from my bad habits and old thought process so that I can start a new life in You. Break the cycles of failure, disobedience and idleness in my life. I'm ready for change. In Jesus' name, Amen.

It's Time For a Revolution!

Every day the enemy is scheming, prowling, strategizing and calculating ways to take you out. Sometimes he will plant a seed to get you agitated or cause you to overreact and burn with anger. Sometimes he will create mass confusion in your job, in your home and in every relationship that matters most to you. His goal is to get you off track but let me tell you something sista girl, it's time to fight back and start a spiritual revolution! The devil doesn't have any new tricks, he just uses new methods to trip you up. Until you begin to take your thoughts captive, everything will seem overwhelming and impossible. But remember, nothing is impossible for God. First, believe you can do this. God says so. Secondly, identify and challenge your old belief system that needs to go. Then, practice healthy habits for a healthy mind. The bible says, "And be not conformed to this world but be transformed by the renewing of your mind."

Romans 12:2 Where the head goes, the body will follow. Practice leads to progress and we are all a work in progress on this side of heaven.

Philippians 4:13 I can do all things through him who strengthens me.

. . . .

. . . .

. . . .

. . . .

. . . .

. . . .

. . . .

Prayer:

Lord help me grow and expand my faith. Help me lean on You because I don't have to fight this battle alone when I have You on my side. Thank You Lord for always being on time. In Jesus name, Amen.

You're Leaking

Sometimes, you don't know you're leaking until someone tells you. I remember when I was nursing our second child and during my lunch break at work, I would go to the daycare to nurse her since my job wasn't far away. I remember one day I was running behind, so I had to hurry to get back to work before pumping the rest of the milk into a bottle for later. When I finally got back to my desk, my co-worker stopped me and said, "Hey your shirt has a large watermark on the front." I was so embarrassed. Sometimes you are moving so quickly through life that you don't even stop to enjoy the moments and sooner than later you are leaking energy and drive. I know what it's like when people expect a lot of you. And you don't want to let anyone down. I know what it's like to just want to bury yourself as you hold back tears and want to scream but you don't. I also know what it's like when you're working a lot harder than others and not catching your break and you are now bursting from every seam. You can't continue to plug holes without eventually fixing the leak. If a clog stays too long, you will experience a water line break.

Joshua 1:9 Have I not commanded you? Be strong and courageous. Do not be frightened, and do not be dismayed, for the Lord your God is with you wherever you go."

. . . .

. . . .

. . . .

. . . .

. . . .

. . . .

. . . .

Prayer:

Heavenly Father, thank You for Your guidance. Your ways are perfect, Lord. Thank You for offering gentle grace and mercy. In Jesus' name, Amen.

DAY 86
Quarantine Your Thoughts

During this year, 2020 we experienced a global pandemic that swept the world. The virus was spreading so fast that the U.S. government required everyone to remain at home until there was a decline in the spread of COVID-19 cases. I never would have thought that being quarantined at home would create the level of anxiety that I was experiencing. Have you ever experienced a sense of mental heaviness that was like a hundred-pound weight? Even if you are not given to fear and doubt, you can be attacked by a spirit of heaviness like I was. When that happens, don't carry it by yourself. Take it to the Lord immediately. Ask a mature believer to pray with you if you need to. Sensing your own limitations doesn't mean you don't have faith. When faith has blossomed, it gives birth to hope and says, "There is an end to this. I won't be in this situation forever. I won't always feel like this. I won't always feel hurt." Hope and faith together give you a vision for your life.

2 Corinthians 10:5 We demolish arguments and every pretension that sets itself up against the knowledge of God, and we take captive every thought to make it obedient to Christ.

· ·

· ·

· ·

· ·

· ·

· ·

· ·

Prayer:

Lord my mind is in need of a reboot. I need a spiritual reawakening. Oftentimes I am in despair because I lose sight of Your plan for my life. Teach me to stay connected to the Rock of my salvation. While we are navigating through these tumultuous times, encourage our hearts and heal our land. In Jesus' name, Amen.

DAY 87
Surrender to Rest

I am the queen of multitasking. But I have to admit, when I try to do too many things at once like texting while driving, talking on the phone while eating and watching television, etc. things tend to fall by the wayside. I believe we have lost an understanding of the brain's need to focus on one thing at a time. Just because you go to sleep, doesn't mean you're actually rested. We all need to take time out of our overscheduled day to just sit still and be quiet. But for those super type A personalities, take advantage of getting quality rest to help you focus when the time is right because when you're well-rested you can engage in complex thinking and strategic problem solving. So, I encourage you to pause, disconnect and get some quality rest. Trust me, whatever it is you think you need to get done, it will be there when you wake up!

Matthew 11:28-30. "Come to me, all who labor and are heavy laden, and I will give you rest.

Isaiah 40:31 But those who hope in the Lord will renew their strength; they will soar on wings like eagles; they will run and not grow weary; they will walk and not be faint."

. . . .

. . . .

. . . .

. . . .

. . . .

. . . .

. . . .

Prayer:

Jesus, I am tired. My mind is frazzled, my hands are full, and my emotions are scattered. Help me to come to You in the midst of being overwhelmed. Remind me of Your ever-present help in my times of need, in Jesus' name, Amen.

DAY 88
Knee Deep

I love the scenery and sound of beaches, but I am not a fan of swimming in the water. I remember the very first time I went to the beach. I was in awe of the expanse of God's creation of the ocean. As far as my eyes could see, there was nothing but water and sky. I was amazed at how awesome it was. I told myself I would just take off my shoes to step in the water and feel the sand between my toes and how cool the waves felt against my skin. In the midst of my awe, I realized the water was getting higher and higher and before I knew it, I was knee deep in the ocean water. At that point, I was all-in and had to make a choice to scurry back to shore or take a swim and enjoy the moment. Have you ever been in a predicament where you didn't want to commit to something but because you said yes to one thing, it turned into something much bigger and more overwhelming than you imagined? It's easy to get caught up in the busyness of life without calculating the risk of overcommitting. Take some time today to reevaluate your commitments so that you can prioritize your life and keep the main thing the "main thing."

Matthew 14:29-30 Then Peter got down out of the boat, walked on the water and came toward Jesus. But when he saw the wind, he was afraid and, beginning to sink, cried out, "Lord, save me!"

. . . .

. . . .

. . . .

. . . .

. . . .

. . . .

. . . .

Prayer:

Lord, Thank You for saving me from things I never knew were potential dangers for me. I confess that I have a tendency to overcommit myself and it can sometimes cause conflict in my relationships with you and with friends and family. Forgive me for being anxious and a busybody. Teach me how to calm down and rest in your presence so that I may gain wisdom, understanding and patience. Amen

Derailments and Detours.

I love taking road trips, but I really don't like driving more than six hours. I know you are probably thinking, that is not a true road trip. I remember, several years ago my husband and I took a road trip to Arkansas. During that time, we used roadmaps on MapQuest, this was pre-Google Maps, or GPS in the vehicle. We had a printed version of our driving directions to help navigate where we needed to be. Nevertheless, we took a wrong turn and got lost in the backwoods of the Ozarks in Arkansas. This trip reminded me of how life can be full of detours, derailments, setbacks and even setups but it's all about how we respond to these situations. During our trip, it would have been easy to just throw in the towel or even say forget it. I'm returning home; but if you turn back too quickly you can miss out on the experience that is waiting for you. So, I encourage you to pause and pray for direction and discernment in the detour and ask the Lord to open your eyes and allow the Holy Spirit to lead. You may be in store for a blessing you never anticipated. There are hidden blessings in every detour.

Exodus 13:17-18, "God did not lead them on the road through the Philistine country, though that was shorter… God led the people around by the desert road toward the Red Sea."

. . . .

. . . .

. . . .

. . . .

. . . .

. . . .

. . . .

Prayer:

Lord, help me to keep my focus on You and Your promises. There are always distractions awaiting me and I am all too willing to look aside and feed my fears, my appetites, and my curiosity. Help me to seek You and find the blessings in the midst of every trial. In Jesus' name, Amen.

Memory Stones

There are some things from the past I wish I could erase. To be honest I think I have unconsciously because they're so painful. Surviving an affair in your marriage can be one of the most traumatic events you can experience, and some psychologists say it's the same physiological experience of losing a loved one. Early in my marriage, my husband had an affair and I felt at that moment you could have just buried me alive six feet under. We can say we were young, didn't have premarital counseling or good counseling, didn't have accountability partners, well we had all of that and yes, we were young but being young is not an excuse for selfishness and disobedience. Affairs don't start over night. There is usually something that broke or fractured way before the incident occurred. But I can tell you, if you're both willing to restore the relationship, you can. Your old ways, old actions and old tendencies must die so call the funeral director, the Holy Spirit to help you with your funeral plans. Surviving an affair requires new rules, new vows, accountability partners, transparency and a lot of time to restore trust and the commitment to talk about all the scary and uncomfortable things. We started incorporating memory stones or reminders of what we will never do again and having an emotional and physical affair was one of them. Each victory was memorized with a stone to remind us never to go back and that old marriage was dead, we are now renewed. It wasn't easy and believe me, many times I wanted to leave and even throw the proverbial stone. We both wanted to throw stones, but we committed to working it out. It was only God who restored my marriage. Memory stones enable us to bring the joys, dreams, and lessons of yesterday into today. As you recall God's faithfulness, you can remain centered and grow. and move forward with a sense of purpose. There is a purpose for your marriage, and it's bigger than you.

Psalm 78:7 So that they should set their hope in God and not forget the works of God, but keep his commandments;

. . . .

. . . .

. . . .

. . . .

. . . .

. . . .

. . . .

Prayer:

Heavenly Father, help us forget the things we need to forget, but remember the things we need to remember. Teach us the kind of selective memory that is healthy for our soul, glorifying to You, and edifying to others. In Jesus' name, Amen.

The Struggle is Real

Praising, shouting, rejoicing is all easy when you're on top and life is amazing and going well. But what do you do when trouble comes (and it will come often)? I would encourage you to praise, not for the struggle but for His presence and to praise Him for His promise to never leave us not forsake us. Give thanks in every situation. You might say, "Well hey I'm human and that's hard when you just had an argument with your spouse and your children are wilding out, you lost your job, your bills and outgo are more than your income, your health has declined, you're in foreclosure on your forever home and the doctor's prognosis doesn't look good. Do I still praise God?" Yes, because in the midst of it all, He still died for you and me and His promise never changes no matter if you praise Him or not. Sometimes you have to shock the enemy and catch him off guard when you praise God in spite of the devil plotting against you. Continue to praise God through your circumstances.

I Thessalonians 5:18 Give thanks in all circumstances; for this is the will of God in Christ Jesus for you.

. . . .

. . . .

. . . .

. . . .

. . . .

. . . .

. . . .

Prayer:

Jesus, thank You for Your sacrifice to save me. I thank You for giving us the promise that You will never leave nor or forsake us. I will rejoice through all my circumstances because I know there is a lesson in the struggle for me to learn, to grow and inspire others. Hallelujah and Amen.

Take Off Your Cape

Sorry to rain on your parade ladies but you are not Superwoman so take off your cape. Early in my career, I used to hoard my vacation days. I did it at first because I didn't want to use sick days with my little kids and then it became a badge of honor. I would tell myself secretly that I was invincible and didn't need to take time off. But now, as a senior leader in my company, I've realized I have become a martyr. With nothing gained except sleepless nights, high anxiety, being over-scheduled and over-extended. No one has it all together all the time. Believe me, something has to eventually fall or break. Even if you can balance and juggle everything at once, let me tell you Sista, there is no such thing as a true work-life balance. When you're looking for so-called work-life balance, you're actually looking for life balance and when it comes to life balance you need a whole lot of grace and a whole lot of mercy. It's okay to remove your cap from time to time. Don't forget to properly prioritize the important things in your life. Think about it, what does every flight attendant tell the passengers before takeoff? They tell you, in the unlikely event that there is a loss of cabin pressure, an oxygen mask will automatically appear and, if traveling with someone who requires assistance, you are instructed to secure your own mask first and then assist the other person. It makes sense—if you don't have enough oxygen, you'll pass out before you can help anybody else.

Newsflash: You are not a superhero. You are going to pass out if you don't take care of yourself! Yes, you're great, fearfully and wonderfully made, but you are still human, and you have limitations. But the God we serve has no limits. Seek Him first.

Psalm 105:4 Look to the Lord and his strength; seek his face always.

Nehemiah 8:10 Do not grieve, for the joy of the Lord is your strength.

Day
92

· ·

· ·

· ·

· ·

· ·

· ·

· ·

Prayer:

Heavenly Father, grant me peace of mind and calm my troubled heart. I can't seem to find my balance, so I stumble and worry constantly. Give me the strength and clarity of mind to find my purpose and walk the path You've laid out for me, in Jesus Name, Amen.

Grow Where You're Planted

My Dad would always tell me "Kiddo you just need to grow where you're planted and just bloom in the season you're in." I don't proclaim that I have a green thumb, but I do know a few things about planting flowers and sowing seeds. Every Spring, I generally plant a new batch of flowers in my flowerbed. Some annuals that will only grow during the Summer and some perennials that will come back every year. Several Summers ago, I went to the home improvement store and I bought this beautiful purple plant with lavender colored flowers. It wasn't labeled and was on clearance so I said what the heck, if it dies, I will at least enjoy it for a season. Surprisingly, it has been coming back every year with more flowers than the previous year. This reminds me of how we should be when we are either in a blooming season or a pruning season. Sometimes life is hard. Things don't always go according to plan. Even in less than wonderful situations, we have control over how we respond. Blooming where we are planted is to make the choice to respond in a positive manner. There are times to bloom where we are planted and times for us to be transplanted so we can bloom even better elsewhere. Just follow the Lord where He leads you.

John 15:5 I am the vine; you are the branches. If you remain in me and I in you, you will bear much fruit; apart from me you can do nothing.

Day

93

. . . .

. . . .

. . . .

. . . .

. . . .

. . . .

. . . .

Prayer:

Lord, You know the season I'm in and the season I'm entering. Help me stay connected to You and rooted in Your word so I can grow and flourish in my due season, in Jesus' name, Amen.

Home Renovations

I am a huge HGTV fan. I can literally watch that channel all day long. I love watching amateurs demo a home or design experts working with homeowners on whether they will keep or sell their home following a full renovation. When God renovates us, He repairs our broken relationships, fixes our broken hearts, replaces dysfunctional attitudes, reinforces good behavior, renews and refreshes our lives. Remodeling and renovating take what already exist and reconfigures it into something different and new. Accepting Christ in your life is like applying a brand-new fresh coat of paint over a dark and dim wall in a room. Once you add primer, you can take any dark room to a fresh and bright new palette. Following Christ requires us to give up certain things in order that we might gain others. Before you conclude that there is too much to give up, consider carefully Christ's important question. "What will you benefit if you gain the whole world but lose your own soul? Is anything worth more than your soul?" Don't just renovate the bedroom, go all in and renovate your entire home.

Joshua 24:15 But as for me and my house, we will serve the Lord.

Hebrews 3:4 For every house is built by someone, but God is the builder of everything.

Day
94

. . . .

. . . .

. . . .

. . . .

. . . .

. . . .

. . . .

Prayer:

God, I believe Your Word to be true and I will align myself accordingly, to ensure total restoration, and transformation of my mind. In Your most sovereign and Holy Name I pray. Amen

I Got Nothing But Love

Sour patch watermelons, fresh mangos, kids, HGTV, the color mustard yellow, cupcakes, yard projects, the sound of ocean waves, cute earrings, cookie dough, reggae music, white sandy beaches and journaling would top my favorite things list in no particular order. There are so many things we do that we don't love or even like because we are seeking the approval from others or trying to fit in. I also love watching romantic comedies and movies with a strong bad a** woman, can I say that even with the asterisks? Well I guess I can since I'm the author of the book. And I absolutely love anything that is gitty, girlie with tons of sprinkles. There comes a moment in life where you just do the things you want to do and absolutely love. Don't you want to live a life full of no regrets? I wrote this journal not because I wanted to but because I needed to. Something is waiting on you to show up. There is something that you have a lot of love, drive and desire for and when you find it your passion will be waiting to greet you.

Isaiah 43:19 See, I am doing a new thing! Now it springs up; do you not perceive it? I am making a way in the wilderness and streams in the wasteland.

Proverbs 19:8 To acquire wisdom is to love oneself; people who cherish understanding will prosper.

. . . .

. . . .

. . . .

. . . .

. . . .

. . . .

. . . .

Prayer:

God, I have a tendency to be cautious and anxious, so I ask You to help me finally believe in myself and go all in. Not blindly but with wisdom, conviction and truth. Remove the mask that I wear so I can embrace the full me, in Jesus' name, Amen.

Break Dancing

As a kid, one of my favorite 80's movies was Breakin' with the main characters, Turbo and Ozone. What I loved most about this movie was the energy and the excitement when they were teaching new people how to breakdance. I have always wanted to learn how to pop-lock or do a fast windmill and walk like a robot. Learning a new skill can be challenging. It's like becoming a new Christ follower. When I gave my life to Christ for the first time, I was 9 years old. Honestly, I don't know if I was moved by the Baptist preacher that Sunday morning or if I just wanted to get dunked in the baptismal pool. Obviously, I became a Christ follower for the wrong reasons, and it wasn't until I was in my early 20's that I rededicated my life and renewed my relationship with God. Let me take this moment for you to rededicate your life to Jesus and renew your faith. Jesus is the best thing in my life because He chose me before I even knew Him. He knew me and loved me even when I was a sinner and I want to share Him with you right now. If you want to accept Jesus as your Lord and Savior, pray this prayer with me, "Jesus I am a sinner and I have tried to do this thing called life by myself and I continue to fail. Lord I know You know my every weakness, but You still love me. Lord, I yield to You and ask that you come into my heart. Lord I believe in You and I believe that You died on the cross for my sins and I believe in Your redemptive blood and Your resurrection power. I surrender my life to you." If you said that prayer, you are saved. The next step is for you to find a local church in your area and get connected with other believers that can come alongside you in your walk with God. If you have said this prayer, please let me know by emailing me at kara@realationships.net. I would love to continue to support you during this amazing journey. Now, friend, let's break dance like nobody's watching. Go all in, have faith and break loose!

Ecclesiastes 3:4 A time to weep and a time to laugh, a time to mourn and a time to dance,

Psalm 149:3 Let them praise his name with dancing and make music to him with timbrel and harp.

. . . .

. . . .

. . . .

. . . .

. . . .

. . . .

. . . .

Prayer:

Heavenly Father, I come to You today to give You all the praise and honor that is due unto You alone. Thank You Lord for saving me and for Your goodness towards us all. In Jesus' name, Amen.

It Will Be Okay

While we sleep, God is still working which is why I can confidently say everything is going to be okay. It might not be ideal at the moment, but it will be okay when it's all said and done. You've made it this far. Clearly, you've been able to survive and overcome many of the obstacles you've faced already. Which probably means you can use those experiences and lessons to face the next obstacles that come your way. Saying it's okay means everything is currently fine. Regardless of whatever happened, it is all good now. Saying it will be okay means things are not good yet, but they will be in the future. Activate your faith and believe that you will be okay because storms don't last forever, and your trials will not last too much longer.

Joshua 1:9 So, no matter how your day goes today, know that God's relationship with you is immovable. Have I not commanded you? Be strong and courageous. Do not be afraid; do not be discouraged, for the Lord your God will be with you wherever you go.

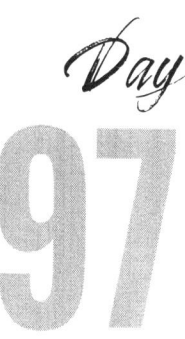

Day

97

· ·

· ·

· ·

· ·

· ·

· ·

· ·

Prayer:

Thank you Lord for being my anchor and my shield during times of trouble and challenges. I thank You for Your presence and Your covering. Help me keep my focus on You, in Jesus' name, Amen.

Hula Hope

Have you ever used a hula hoop as a kid? Many of us probably thought that it was solely the hips that kept the hula hoop from falling but it actually is the combination of your hips with your abdomen. To keep a hula hoop spinning you have to create momentum when rocking back and forth pushing your hips and belly forward, slightly shifting your weight as it spins around your waist. Hope is like a hula hoop. "How is that?" Well I'm glad you asked. The reason hope is like a hula hoop is because it's the combination of discipline and determination to believe in God's word and His promises even when the world seems to be crashing all around you. Hope combined with faith will create the momentum and rhythm you need to win. If you can hold on and keep your faith, the Lord will be with you every step of the way throughout your life especially when you need Him most. He will be your guide. Faith is an action verb, it is about believing, listening, and acting out the word of God. The deeper you dive into God's word, the deeper your faith will grow. So, start hula hooping and apply your hope and faith in Jesus today.

Romans 10:17 "So faith comes from hearing, and hearing through the word of Christ."

Day

98

. . . .

. . . .

. . . .

. . . .

. . . .

. . . .

. . . .

Prayer:

Lord, help me keep my faith and not get weary in doing so. Help me stay focused rooted and grounded in You. In Jesus' name, Amen.

Chosen and Accepted

One of my favorite worship songs is "Who You Say I Am" by Hillsong Worship. The lyrics say, "I am chosen, not forsaken. I am who You say I am. You are for me; Not against me. I am who You say I am." It doesn't matter what they say about you or who you think you are. What matters is who God says who you are. You are wanted, valued, chosen and accepted. I remember when my oldest daughter was looking at colleges during high school. She was accepted into many schools, but she could only choose one and the one she really wanted didn't offer enough scholarship money to attend. It's a great feeling when you're selected or accepted. However, it's a different feeling when you're rejected and looked over. But let me remind you that although you may feel rejected, demoted, cast away, let go, or even released, God chose you, yes you. Beloved, you are worthy because God made you worthy and you are accepted because of Jesus Christ.

1 Peter 2:9 But you are a chosen generation, a royal priesthood, a holy nation, His own special people, that you may proclaim the praises of Him who called you out of darkness into His marvelous light.

. . . .

. . . .

. . . .

. . . .

. . . .

. . . .

. . . .

Prayer:

Jesus, thank You for accepting me even when I often reject You and Your word. I am grateful that You have never left me, and You choose me even when I haven't always chosen You. In You I'm accepted, not rejected. Thank you for your grace and mercy, in Jesus' name, Amen.

Today is Your Day

New beginnings are all around you and within you every day. You don't need to wait for a clean slate to start something new. You can conquer the moment today. God is in the business of making all things new. His healing brings restoration beyond understanding, no matter where you come from or what you've done. You made it to day 100 and I applaud your commitment. Now I know you probably skipped to this page just to see how the journal ends, and that's ok. But no matter what order you read this book, you are reading this day and I want to tell you, Today is your Day! Today is the day to start or restart your journey. Today is the day you begin believing that you have greatness inside you. Today is the day that you begin to cast your net out farther because your vision is bigger than you. Today is the day that you create new healthy habits and patterns in your life. Today is your day to be who you were called and destined to be. Yes, you may slip, or you may fall but today is the day that you pull your shoulders back, stand like you are balancing a pineapple on the top of your head and walk with authority and grace. Today is your day to be the best version of you. I am so proud of you. I just want to tell you that in case no one has. You are awesome and amazing.

Matthew 17:20 He said to them, "Because of your little faith. For truly, I say to you, if you have faith like a grain of mustard seed, you will say to this mountain, 'Move from here to there,' and it will move, and nothing will be impossible for you."

. . . .

. . . .

. . . .

. . . .

. . . .

. . . .

. . . .

Prayer:

Lord, I have made a decision to follow You. I know You hear my prayers even if I don't see the answers right away. No matter what happens, I am certain that I am not without hope. Lord, strengthen my faith where it is weak. I put my life in Your hands. In Jesus' name, Amen.

This journal is dedicated to Bear, my husband, my love and best friend.